Youth Ministry in
Papua New Guinea

Youth Ministry in Papua New Guinea

Challenge, Theology, and Curriculum

Danijela Schubert

WIPF & STOCK · Eugene, Oregon

YOUTH MINISTRY IN PAPUA NEW GUINEA
Challenge, Theology, and Curriculum

All scripture quotations, unless otherwise indicated, are taken from the Holy Bible, New International Version®, NIV®. Copyright ©1973, 1978, 1984, 2011 by Biblica, Inc.™ Used by permission of Zondervan. All rights reserved worldwide. www.zondervan.com The "NIV" and "New International Version" are trademarks registered in the United States Patent and Trademark Office by Biblica, Inc.™

Copyright © 2013 Danijela Schubert. All rights reserved. Except for brief quotations in critical publications or reviews, no part of this book may be reproduced in any manner without prior written permission from the publisher. Write: Permissions, Wipf and Stock Publishers, 199 W. 8th Ave., Suite 3, Eugene, OR 97401.

Wipf & Stock
An Imprint of Wipf and Stock Publishers
199 W. 8th Ave., Suite 3
Eugene, OR 97401

www.wipfandstock.com

ISBN 13: 978-1-62564-053-6

Manufactured in the U.S.A.

To my husband Branimir and sons Filip and Timotei,
who always encouraged me to complete this project

Contents

Acknowledgments | ix
Introduction | xi

Part 1: Youth Ministry Challenge in PNG
1 Context | 3
2 Psychosocial Development | 19
3 Influences and Ecology | 34

Part 2: Youth Ministry as Practical Theology in the SDA Context
4 Biblical Call of Adoption and Practical Theology | 59
5 Youth Ministry History in the SDA Church | 72
6 Anticipated Trends | 82

Part 3: Curriculum for Introduction to Youth Ministry Course
7 Course Goals and Learning Outcomes | 95
8 Elements of the Curriculum | 102

Summary and Conclusion | 111
Appendices
  A *Selected Bibliography for Introduction to Youth Ministry Course* | 117
  B *Sample Lesson Studies* | 119
Bibliography | 127

Acknowledgments

FIRST OF ALL I acknowledge God, who I believe should take full credit for my success.

I believe this book, based on my doctoral work, would not have been finished if so many people did not pray for me, encourage me, and believe in me. First of all my close relatives: my mother Štefica Bratulić, my sister Marija Đidara, and my parents-in-law Velimir and Mariana Šubert. Such support I also received from friends, I will mention a few only: Aila Stammler, Camille Bennetts, Dora Iro, Younis and Romina Masih.

I would like to thank Pacific Adventist University (PAU), especially the School of Theology for allowing me to have a reduced workload while pursuing my doctoral degree. I am also grateful for their financial support in paying my airfares. Appreciation also goes to my colleagues at PAU: David Tasker, who spurred me on to further study, David Thiele, Graeme Humble, Jennifer Jones, Tracie Mafile'o, and others.

I thank my DMin cohort colleagues: Andrea Trusty-King, Christopher Pollock, Chuck Hunt, Jim Byrne, John Tan, Kelly Lashley, Lance Bourgeois, Mark Sheets, Nick Kross, and Paul Walker, who made it look like it is just fun. I acknowledge Chap Clark, our professor, who led us through this journey, gave me the idea of writing the original paper, and trusted that I could do it.

I appreciate the assistance of the South Pacific Division of the Seventh-day Adventist Church administration for the grant and three weeks of paid study leave.

Acknowledgments

I am grateful to Sonya Muhl for editing my paper. It has been a great help in a short time.

Finally, although I have dedicated this book to my husband and sons, I would like to acknowledge them again. They believed in me, helped read and edit my assignments throughout the years of study, gave suggestions, cooked meals, helped me up when I was down, and handled my frustrations. I am so blessed to have such a lovely family and friends around me.

Introduction

TWO HUNDRED YEARS AGO, and as recently as 1945, in many parts of Papua New Guinea (PNG), cannibalism was prevalent. Killing a man was needed "in order to wear particular bird plumes in dances or to be part of a male initiation cult . . . [since] men were headhunters, and competed with one another for status by seeking to earn reputation as homicides."[1] Land was considered of high value and generally used in subsistence farming. It belonged to the clan and not an individual. However, "through the 1970s, cattle raising and coffee growing resulted in an increased exclusion of land from subsistence horticultural use."[2] "Land has become the source of new and more complex disputes in PNG in recent years,"[3] even tribal wars that can last for years, even decades.[4] Change was occurring.

In 2003, mobile phones were first introduced in PNG. In 2007, a second mobile phone provider was allowed to do business. Today mobile phones are found not only in the city centres, but also in remote rural areas. Those who can afford it can also have internet access via mobile phone. They can recharge their electricity meters, check their bank balance and send money to a friend's mobile phone to top up their credit, send text messages, and post messages on Facebook, all through a mobile phone. This is perceived as progress for PNG, allowing much better communication between family, friends, and businesses. However, "it is also ironic

1. Eric Hirsch, "Making Up," 241.
2. George Westermark, "Clan Claims," 221.
3. Ibid., 218.
4. Rosita Henry, "Smoke," 431–43.

Introduction

that these developments that come in the name of progress and by implication lifting living standards often accentuate poverty and break down family life by increase in alcohol, sex work and HIV & AIDS, and create larger disparities in wealth within the resource affected areas."[5]

The previous three paragraphs briefly illustrate the rapid change occurring in PNG. This change seems to be impacting the values of society. What was previously not part of the culture, such as out-of-marriage pregnancies, divorce, and promiscuity, are growing in number, and criminal violence seems to be the norm in urban centres. The number of youth suicides is on the rise, car accidents and violence due to alcohol and drug abuse are increasing, and HIV/AIDS figures are alarming, although no clear statistics are available.[6] These changes are influencing the whole society, including churches.

Pastors in PNG are increasingly encountering new issues in working with youth. They are facing unprecedented changes resulting from rapid development and resource-driven economic growth. It appears the almost "overnight" availability of mobile phones, internet, and cable TV is shaping the population of PNG, creating new questions to deal with, particularly in the work with youth. It is especially youth that are vulnerable in this rapidly changing society. They are torn between the traditions their parents are trying to uphold and the changes that industrialization is bringing to PNG. It appears that the pace and the scope of change are reshaping the nation's ethos.

Since the change is very rapid and spreading further and further inland to remote areas, the challenge of ministering to youth who are under the influence of Western media is urgent. A few

---

5. NASFUND, "Land Owner Management around Resource Projects Need to Be Handled with Sensitivity," October 18, 2010 (e-newsletter).

6. The estimated number of people (of all ages) living with HIV in 2007 was fifty-four thousand. UNICEF, "At a Glance: Papua New Guinea: Statistics," online: http://www.unicef.org/infobycountry /papuang_statistics.html, accessed October 18, 2010. AusAID predicts that by 2012 there will be over 208,000 living with HIV. "HIV/AIDS in Papua New Guinea," online: http://www.ausaid.gov.au/country/png/hivaids.cfm, accessed October 18, 2010.

Introduction

years ago, this may have been a challenge only in the major cities, but today it has spread much farther. Remote areas of PNG may not have running water or electricity, but may have numerous television channels brought by satellite, run on solar-powered electricity, and use mobile phones with internet connections. Relatives who come for a visit may bring laptops with them with pictures and movies that will amaze the local population. However, having had no background in this mode of communication, they have no developed systems for coping with and evaluating its influence.

Pastors are often the most educated people in the village community. The church and people rely on them to bring needed understanding and balance to the society. In order to provide this kind of service, they need to be equipped for the task of working with youth who are confronted with these changes, while at the same time struggling with old animistic/cultural traditions. They need to acquire knowledge about youth work from Western countries as the same issues are now affecting the PNG youth. They also need to take into account the local circumstances specific to the youth of PNG. Their plans and programs must be based on sound biblical theology.

The purpose of this book is to present a curriculum for a master's-level course—Introduction to Youth Ministry— taught in PNG and aimed at pastors and youth workers, that is biblically based and contextually relevant. The book contains three major sections. The first part deals with the youth ministry challenge in PNG by discussing three main issues: the context, psychosocial development, and influences and ecology.

Chapter 1 describes the context of PNG society based on the area in which a citizen lives. Whether a person grew up or lives in a village, the city, an island, or the Highlands will have a great impact on their worldview, habits, language, and even personal features. Chapter 2 identifies the psychosocial development of youth as seen in Melanesian cultures and also the psychosocial development as described in Western societies. It points out the characteristics of both and the changes that are occurring in both views. Chapter 3 addresses the influences on the youth of PNG,

xiii

Introduction

looking into media influences such as radio, TV, music, the Internet, and print, pointing out the fast changes in society brought with the recent "invasion" of Western media. It also looks at the influence of family, both immediate, extended, and *wantok* system, as well as the role that the animistic background plays.

The second part of this book discusses youth ministry as practical theology in the Seventh-day Adventist (SDA) context. This part gives an overview of the biblical call of adoption, as well as practical theology, youth ministry history, and anticipated trends in the practice of youth ministry. Chapter 4 assesses the biblical call of adoption by giving an overview of the biblical view of family and youth ministry. This theology is based on both the Old and New Testaments, and identifies the most significant and distinctive aspects of Adventism to indicate how they influence the approach to practical ministry with youth. This theology is limited to the SDA view of eschatology, with its roots based in the United States and the form of governance the SDA church has transported around the world. Chapter 5 briefly discusses the history of youth ministry in the SDA church. It looks at the general development of youth ministry as originated in the United States and then portrays the same process in PNG. Chapter 6 develops the anticipated trends in youth ministry in the SDA church and their possible impact in PNG.

The third part of this book offers a suggested curriculum for a master's level course, Introduction to Youth Ministry. Two chapters cover course goals with learning outcomes and elements of the curriculum. Chapter 7 proposes the course goals and learning outcomes. It is specific to the PNG context, based on the information provided in part one and two of this document. Chapter 8 provides elements of the curriculum. It has information on the major units of the course, explanation of the assignments required from the students, and the instruments of measuring the performance of individual students. The appendix contains sample lesson plans.

For the past nine years, I have lectured in the School of Theology, where student diversity ranged from high school dropouts to fifty-year-olds, and all ages in between. As a Sabbath school teacher I have worked with teenagers (twelve- to eighteen-year-olds) for

Introduction

the past four years. During the same period I have been a mother of two teenage sons. From the experiences I encountered in the classroom, Sabbath school, dialogue with parents and colleagues, and conversations at home, I am aware of the challenges PNG faces with its young population. This project will help those training to be leaders in the community to find ways of turning these challenges into opportunities.

PART 1

Youth Ministry Challenge in PNG

CHAPTER 1

Context

TO UNDERSTAND THE MESSAGE of the Bible, one needs to understand the context in which the Bible was written: where, why, and to whom it was written. This is now the commonly accepted view of understanding its content. Similarly, to decide how to transmit its message, one needs to understand the context—to whom and where it is to be passed on—and then to decide how to do that. Chapter 1 describes the context of the PNG society based on the area in which a citizen might live. Whether a person grew up or lives in a village or the city, an island or the Highlands, will have a great impact on their worldview, habits, language, and even personal characteristics.

Papua New Guinea is a country just south of the equator, about 150 kilometers north of the tip of Australia, between the Bismarck and Coral Seas in the South Pacific Ocean. On its western side, it has a land border of 820 kilometers with Indonesia, which occupies the other half of the island of New Guinea. It is the largest country in the South Pacific, except for Australia. PNG has over six hundred islands, but the main landmass, referred to as mainland, is on New Guinea. PNG occupies an area of 462,840 square kilometers, of which 9,980 is water. Its coastline is 5,152 kilometers.

Part 1: Youth Ministry Challenge in PNG

PNG is divided administratively into twenty-two provinces.[1] These divisions are more than administrative—for example, there is no road suitable for vehicles connecting the two neighboring provinces Central and Milne Bay. Although PNG has over 19,600 kilometers of roads, only 686 kilometers are sealed. Similarly, out of 571 airports, only twenty-one have sealed runways.[2] The climate, although tropical, shows great diversity between provinces. A stark example is the annual rainfall. Milne Bay region, for example, receives over 5,000 millimeters of rain annually, and the delta region of Fly River, close to 6,000 millimeters, while Port Moresby, although situated in between the two, only receives about 1,150 millimeters annually.[3] About 98 percent of the people are Melanesian, other groups include Polynesian, Micronesian, Chinese, and European. Politically, the divisions are Papuans, Highlanders, New Guineans, and Islanders.[4] For a country that is comparable in size to California, the population of just over six million people (2012 estimate) makes it sparsely populated. However, although statistically not densely populated, in some cities and households the population is very dense: there could be twenty people sleeping in a two-bedroom house in the city.

Even though PNG is by constitution a Christian country, it is at the same time an independent and free country, with other religions, like Islam, Buddhism, and Baha'i, present in small numbers. When meeting another person on the street, it is safe to assume that the other is a Christian from one of the predominant denominations. The main religion is Catholic, followed by Lutherans. In the 2000 census, approximately 10 percent of the population have

---

1. Bougainville, Central, Chimbu, Eastern Highlands, East New Britain, East Sepik, Enga, Gulf, Hela, Jiwaka, Madang, Manus, Milne Bay, Morobe, National Capital District, New Ireland, Northern, Sandaun, Southern Highlands, Western, Western Highlands, West New Britain.

2. "Papua New Guinea,"*About.com*, accessed September 14, 2010, online: http://geography.about.com/library/cia/blcpapua.htm.

3. "Papua New Guinea," *Microsoft Encarta Reference Library 2007*, DVD-ROM.

4. Ibid.

Context

declared themselves Seventh-day Adventists, although church data reports only half as many members.[5]

PNG boasts an abundance of natural resources, but people are its greatest asset. The variety of cultures, all expressed in unique traditions, art, war preparations (now mostly reenacted), dances, and songs are a real treasure. More than eight hundred different spoken languages are evidence of this diversity. Other great natural resources are rich coral seas abundant in marine life, virgin rain forests in which new species of flora and fauna are still being discovered, an abundance of fresh water from rains, lakes, and rivers, a variety of habitats, gold (one of the finest in the world), liquefied natural gas, and many more. People grow up in these diverse places. They are divided into four contexts in this book: villages, cities, islands, and highlands. The following describes how these contexts influence the worldview of its inhabitants.

Village

Over 80 percent of the population of PNG lives in a village setting. Most of them are subsistence farmers. Life would be very different in a village situated on a small atoll island as compared with the highlands of PNG. For example, an island village would rely on fish, coconut, cassava, banana, breadfruit, sweet potato, and sago for food, building houses, and even clothing. Formal employment is not prevalent.[6] On the other hand, a village in the highlands would rely on sweet potato as the main source of food, but sometimes also English potato, a variety of beans, cabbage, carrots, onions, and other vegetables, bananas, and other fruit, which can be harvested two to three times a year. It is possible to find employment,

---

5. "South Pacific Division, Statistical Report, Annual—Membership for the Year 2007," *Record*, June 14, 2008, supplemental insert, n.p. This is a once-a-year insert in the weekly official paper of the South Pacific Division of the Seventh-day Adventist Church. Although SDA Church membership has been growing, the 2007 report shows less than half the membership of the country's 2000 census declarations.

6. Guy, "Traditional," 42.

Part 1: Youth Ministry Challenge in PNG

at least seasonally, in the large coffee plantations, but some cash income could come from the sale of homegrown food crops not used for family consumption.[7] Cash in the village is scarce and used for purchasing medicine, clothing, and food from the local store, like rice, tinned fish, biscuits, and noodles. Travel expenses and school fees are also paid from the same source. For garden-grown foods a barter system is still used in many villages. Coastal villagers can exchange fish for fruits and sweet potato from the inland villagers.[8]

In the village, the whole community is involved in raising children. Uncles, aunties, cousins and grandparents are all included. While children are young, mothers feed and bathe them, but older siblings or aunties would spend much time with the child, allowing the mother to perform other duties like gardening, cooking, or even working. Such jobs as changing nappies, feeding, or bathing the baby would be the sole domain of women. When boys reach puberty, they are separated from their mothers and spend significant time with their fathers and other males in the village without mixing with women.

Each village would have a men's house where women are not allowed. In villages women also have their house apart from the home, where they stay while menstruating, and no men would enter that place. Village homes are made from bush materials and need regular repairs. They are characterized by small sleeping quarters, soil or sometimes wooden floors, and scarcely any furniture. A traditional village house in the highlands is a thatched-roof building with just one room and an open fireplace in the middle. Some have a small window, and smoke rises from the thatched roof when the fire is burning. Walls are made of wood or woven

---

7. Khambu, "Miruma," 64–67.

8. A few days prior to writing this chapter, a former student, a missionary in a remote area of PNG on the Sepik River, shared this story with me in my office. He thought he would purchase the necessary food in the village where he would live, but garden food is not for sale, only for exchange with some other food from inland villagers. His first duty was to clear some land for a garden where he would grow vegetables and to buy a net so he could do some fishing. In the meantime, he had to rely on the generosity of villagers and some commercial food like white rice and tinned fish that he could purchase from the store.

pitpit leaves. The whole family sleeps inside around the fire place, including the family dog. Those who can afford it use commercial materials to build their homes, as they are more durable. Those houses have roofs and outside walls made of tin. It appears that the lower the altitude where villages are situated, the more often houses are built on stilts, to allow air circulation during the day while it is hot, although some houses in the islands, where it is the hottest, are not built on stilts. The space underneath the stilt houses is where children play and families gather for meals and rest, while at night they sleep inside the house.

Traditionally, girls spend time with their grandmothers, mothers, and aunties, while boys do the same with their grandfathers, fathers, and uncles. From them they learn about life, acquire skills, and prepare for adulthood. Girls learn how to cook, grow food in the gardens, clean the house, raise children, and make *bilums* (string bags) and mats, while boys learn how to clear an area for gardening, how to fight, how to make a house, and how to hunt. If the village is near water, they will also learn how to make a boat and acquire the skills necessary for fishing. The village boys also learn how to use sorcery, which is perceived as beneficial for daily living.[9]

City

The cities of PNG are growing and the country is becoming increasingly urbanized. The influx of people coming from villages to the cities is constant and growing, but immigration is another factor in this growth. Immigrants are from Australia, Sri Lanka, India, China, Philippines, Indonesia, Solomon Islands, and other countries. Increasing opportunities for financial benefit is the main reason for this growth. The two biggest cities are the nation's capital, Port Moresby, and Lae, in Morobe province. Although Port Moresby has more than double the population, Lae has far greater

---

9. Guy, "Traditional," 46.

port activity.[10] Other urban areas are much smaller, generally not exceeding the population of thirty thousand.[11]

The coastal cities, like Port Moresby, have a different style of accommodation. There are suburbs, like Koki and Hanuabada, that are entirely built on stilts above the sea. Their inhabitants rely fully on their income from formal employment to sustain their families. They have no arable land, so they cannot grow any food. They have to buy it all. They have to pay for electricity, education, and clothing. All of that is more expensive in the city than inland. Port Moresby is the most expensive city in PNG, however, it also has the most employment and education opportunities. Another style of accommodation in other parts of the city is either single-house or multiple-apartment dwellings. Those that live in single-house dwellings could make small gardens from which to grow food; however, fresh fruits and vegetables come to Port Moresby from the surrounding areas or highlands. Due to transport costs the prices are significantly higher.

In the city, parents and their children live in a home often shared with other relatives. One room may be given to one family consisting of father, mother, and two or more children, while another room is used by another blood-related family. They may use one kitchen for all. Fathers, and increasingly mothers, too, are out of home, busy with work in formal or informal employment, and there is no wider community to look after children who are left alone. Those that can afford to pay the fees send their children to kindergartens and schools. On any day in downtown Port Moresby, one can see those whose parents cannot afford school fees begging in the streets, sitting and doing nothing, or getting into mischief. Similar to Western societies, children are

---

10. The population of Port Moresby from figures in the 2000 census was 254,158, while Lae's population was around 120,000. The year 2010 census will show the actual increase, but there is no doubt that the increase was significant. Port Moresby port has throughput of 45,000 20 ft. containers, while Lae, 100,000. "Shipping," in *Pacific Economic Survey 2008*, 73.

11. *Wikipedia*, s.v. "List of Cities and Towns in Papua New Guinea by Population," accessed September 15, 2010, online: http://en.wikipedia.org/wiki/List_of_cities_and_towns_in_Papua_New_Guinea_by_population.

Context

left to fend for themselves, or as Chap Clark puts it, they have been "systemically abandoned."[12] Many who come from villages to the city to find a better life end up being unemployed with no shelter or food. Some turn to crime and violence and harm the rest of the society. They are given the name *raskols*. Often they operate as gangs similar to those in Western societies. Many of the younger ones are school dropouts because they are not able to pay the school fees or there simply are not enough spaces in high schools for them. To illustrate how it is to grow up in a city, a first-year student at Pacific Adventist University volunteered to share memories of growing up in Port Moresby. The following paragraphs are derived from that conversation.[13]

A girl living in Port Moresby could spend a day inside four walls. Streets of Port Moresby are not safe playgrounds for girls; newspapers daily report assaults, rapes, burglaries, and killings. The safest place is inside the house or apartment, although the house is no stranger to violence either—she witnessed her father beating her stepmother.

Typically, a house would be equipped with running water, electricity, a kitchen with a gas stove and a fridge, or even a microwave oven, a bathroom with a shower and toilet, and perhaps a television. The family may own a car, a computer, mobile phone, mp3 player, and speakers. A day could be spent watching television. Interesting programs on EMTV (free-to-air channel) might be "Ice Discovered" (local version of "American Idol"), "Who Wants to Be a Millionaire" (from Australia), "Pyramid" (quiz program for students), or the daily news. Most of these are seasonal and short, so if there is nothing else to watch on local television, one could borrow videos, listen to music, or share stories with others in the house. Perhaps she could amuse herself by practicing the skill of sewing a *meri blaus* (local dress) that she learned in school. It would be a girl's job to clean the house, using chemicals and cleaning cloths purchased from the store. She would also wash the

12. Clark and Clark, *Disconnected*, 70–82.

13. Germaine Anivai, interview by author, September 23, 2010, Pacific Adventist University, Port Moresby, PNG.

family's clothes in a twin-tub washing machine. However, most of her free time she would spend studying.

Her day would start by an alarm, and she would want to set it early because it could be that, in this household, there are twenty other persons sleeping and wanting to use the toilet and shower. All the other people are her relatives: parents, siblings, step-parents or step-siblings, cousins, aunties, and uncles. They could be relatives from her mother's or father's side of the family. If the house is on stilts, the upper floor might be used for her family while the rooms underneath could be rented out to yet another six to ten people also from extended families. She would prepare her own breakfast. If the family has a car, her dad could drop her off at school and later in the day pick her up. If not, she would need to walk for about fifteen minutes to catch a bus, and then another fifteen minutes from the bus to her school. She might attend a girls-only school, a private or government run school. When she returns home she would like to study, but family chores might take precedence. There is much chopping and cutting to do to prepare the evening meal, and afterwards there are piles of dishes to be washed. With so many people in the house there is no peace and quiet, which she needs in order to study, so she might go outside on the balcony and try hard to concentrate. After dinner they might have a family fellowship where she would take part in reading the Scriptures, leading the singing, and praying. By ten o'clock, she would go to bed in a room shared with many other people.

All that she and her family eat would be food purchased from markets and stores. Those family members who are employed and earn wages would be the ones purchasing the food and paying for electricity, gas, school fees, medical and travel expenses, and any other costs. However, when one of them would visit family in the village, they could bring some food back from the village to help with the food bill. Their food would consist of white rice, chicken, vegetables, greens, and garden food.

Throughout her childhood, she might live in several houses from one side of the city to the other. Housing is often dependent on one's job. If the father works for a company, that company could

Context

provide a house. If he stops working for the company, he will need to vacate the house. If he finds another job with a house they could move there, but if not, they will rely on the hospitality of their relatives and move in with them. She may need to move houses, also, depending on the family situation. If the parents are separated or divorced, she may live with one of them. If one of them should die, hopefully the other one will accept the responsibility of raising her and her siblings or even half-siblings.

Islands

PNG has over six hundred islands. Some of them are large, like New Britain, New Ireland, and Bougainville, while others are very small, like Pahi Island, west of Manus, in the Admiralty Islands region. Large islands have enough land and fresh water, similar to people living on the mainland of PNG. Those on small islands have less arable land and must rely on other sources for survival. Many islands are small and birds may be their only inhabitants. Residents of Manus Island were among the earliest islanders in PNG who decided to send their brightest children to schools. With good education, it was thought, they would get good jobs and support their parents and the rest of their family with their salaries.[14] A first-year education student at Pacific Adventist University shared his memories of growing up on the Feni Islands.[15] The following paragraphs are derived from his stories.[16]

How one will experience growing up on an island depends on whether the child is a boy or a girl, whether the child attends school or not, whether it is a dry season or rainy season, and on the other siblings in the family. A girl would need to work in the

14. Gustafsson, "Poverty," 30–31.
15. Another name for it is Anir Island. For a brief description of the island, see "Come and See Amazing Anir," *Island News*, October 2008, accessed September 27, 2010, online: http://www.lglgold.com/data/portal/00000005/content/61923001227064001713.pdf.
16. Aquino Saklo, interview by author, September 26, 2010, Pacific Adventist University, Port Moresby, PNG.

garden, help with the food preparation and cooking, collect firewood, and help with the dishes. If there are no female siblings in a family, a boy would need to help the mother with those duties; however, if there are other female siblings, the boys would be mixing with other boys fishing or hunting, swimming, and diving in the sea. A girl might learn from her mother how to make mats from *pandana* (pandanus) leaves. They would go together to collect them and then spend many hours weaving them through to make a *pandana* mat. The family needs the mats to be placed on a bamboo bed for more comfortable sleeping.

It is likely that a boy would be in school on a school day, while a mother may keep her daughter at home to help her with chores and to teach her how to take care of the household. If the boy is at the age of leaving his mother for special education by the elders, he would spend about a year in a men's house, fully occupied with duties assigned to him by the elders, and would not mix with women or girls during that time. They would not even consume food that a female had prepared.

If a boy is in a man's house, his day would start when an elder would wake him up. He would probably not have a bath; sometimes he would not have a bath for several weeks. For breakfast there would be taro roasted on fire, and then the day's activities would begin and would occupy the whole day. Perhaps the day would be fishing and he would be taught how to fish with a spear or with a string. It would be reef fishing, where he would walk in the shallow waters of the beach and try to catch a fish, or he would learn how to paddle a canoe further away to the nearby atoll and fish there using similar techniques. Another time it would be the night fishing. Perhaps between 7:00 p.m. and 9:00 p.m. he would light up coconut *trons* (torch), walk along the reef, and search for fish in the lagoon. The fish that he would catch he would learn how to clean, cover with salt, and leave in the sun to dry. This fish would not be cooked, as it is believed it would lose its energy. It would be eaten raw during the evening meal together with roast taro or *kaukau* (sweet potato). Alternatively, he would catch a special kind of fish which would be smoked and kept for visitors or for

Context

the community to enjoy on special days like weddings, funerals, or when they build a new men's house, as these are big celebrations.

If fishing is not planned for the day, perhaps hunting is. He would learn how to hunt the cuscus and wild pigs with a spear or with special traps. For cuscus he might need to climb trees, as that is where they can be more easily found. If the hunt is at night, he would learn how to hunt for wild fowls and sometimes cuscus.

Climbing trees would not be a problem for a boy on this island. He would climb trees daily, especially coconut trees. Coconut juice would be his favorite drink and he would drink it daily. Coconut flesh would also be his daily food. His dad could have coconut plantations from which some money would come to the family by selling copra.

If it is rainy season, there would be plenty of fresh water collected in the water tank for his family to drink. If it is dry season, he would feel very blessed, since his family lives near a river. Other villages that do not have a river near them would move to the part of the island where water is available. His village of about twenty families would make sure that the rules of using the river water are clear to newcomers so that the river would not be polluted. For drinking water during the dry season he would need to go to the bush and fetch water from far away. He would not consider that a difficult chore.

It is very possible that he might not go to the special training in the men's house. He might be one of the boys in the family who would go to school instead to learn to read and write. He would spend his third to eighth year in the local primary school, which would be about two hours' walk away from his village. Certainly seeing other boys learn how to read and write would spark an interest in him to do the same. He may declare to his father that he wants to go to school, and the father would be happy to send him.

If he were to continue his studies, he would need to go away from his island, away from his parents and relatives to another island where he would be in a boarding school. That would be a very hard time in his life. Learning about so many new things he never knew existed or were important, like money, would cause many

13

Part 1: Youth Ministry Challenge in PNG

questions to swirl in his head: What is money for? How does one use it? What are computers? What is one meant to do with them and how? Are there really people who eat three times a day and have daily showers? How far is the beach where I can dive in?

At least one thing from his previous experiences would come in handy—his knowledge of English. During the last few years, when foreigners came to moor in the atolls near his village for about three weeks, he loved spending time with them, and being the tour guide on his island, otherwise he would not speak English. He has his own language and his dad may be involved in translating the Bible into that language.

His home is made up of bush materials, with separate rooms for females and males. It is a house not built on stilts but level with the ground. At night his father would often sleep outside as a sign of protection of his family. The family would not need covers at night as the temperature is always pleasant, but if they needed warmth they could always make a fire and sleep close to it or have a light cover over them. In the men's house, though, there are no rooms, it is all a big open space.

Feni Islands are made up of two islands joined together with about four villages: Natong, Warambana, Pikan, and Balim. It takes three days' walk to cross to the other side of the island. Plenty of food is grown on the island: taro, yam, sweet potato, *aibika* (green leafy vegetable in PNG), and other greens; pawpaw, guava, mango, bananas, and breadfruit; but the staple food is fish and taro. To get to this island one would need to fly from Port Moresby to Kavieng, travel six hours in a vehicle to the tip of the mainland, and then spend another four hours in a dinghy. For a person who grew up on Feni Island, the long trip is worth taking.

Highlands

Although some of the larger islands of PNG have mountains of up to 2400 m above sea level, like Mt. Gilaut in New Ireland, they are not usually seen as highlands. When the term "highlander" is used, it usually means someone from the mainland from one of the five highland provinces: Eastern, Western and Southern Highlands, Hela, Jiwaka, Chimbu, and Enga. When the Western explorers traversed today's PNG territory, they did not know this fertile plateau existed. Explorations inland before 1930 assumed when they reached the mountains, whether they started from the south or from the north of New Guinea, that those mountains were one range, not two with a plateau in between. It was only in the twentieth century that a huge plateau was discovered with some two million inhabitants who had never seen a white man before. These inhabitants were called the Highlanders. The highest mountain in PNG, Mt. Wilhelm at 4509 m, is in Chimbu Province. The main cities in the highlands are Goroka, Wabag, Mt. Hagen, Mendi, and Kundiawa. A second year nursing student at Pacific Adventist University volunteered to share his childhood memories of growing up in a highlands village. The following paragraphs are derived from his discourse.[17]

A day in the Ku village in Chimbu for a school-age boy would start with daylight. From Monday to Friday during the school year, a simple daily routine would exist. In case daylight did not wake him up, his mother would. She would already be preparing breakfast. He would need nourishment because soon he would walk the four to five kilometres to school. His mother would also be getting his lunch ready. He would probably use the outside toilet and run down to wash his face in the very cold creek water. Before he would leave, he would check the family goat. He would make sure that the rope around its foot is in place and that the other end of the rope is securely tightened around a bush or a small tree. When the sun would be up, or if it would start to rain, somebody would have to take the goat to a shelter they would have built for it.

On the way to school, sometimes he would climb a tree, securely hide his lunch, and with cheeky anticipation wait all day in school, thinking of the lunch waiting for him up that tree. On most days, however, he would bring lunch to school where another three to four hundred children attend. They would all be in grades one to eight, as it is a primary school. The lunch break would be a time

17. Ishmael Yani, interview by author, September 20, 2010, Pacific Adventist University, Port Moresby, PNG.

to play with other children. He would also share his lunch with those who did not have any. School would start at eight o'clock, and would finish by three o'clock. His school bag would be somewhat lighter then, as his lunch would have been eaten, and only exercise books would be left. He would know that somewhere along the path back home he would have to find some firewood to carry home. Sometimes he really would not feel like going to school, but he would know that if he would come back without attending school his mother and father would be very angry with him.

His chores would be waiting for him when he arrived. These would include working in either the garden on the hill where vegetables would be grown or the one near the creek where they would have coffee plants, bananas, and *pandanas*. If there was no water in the house he would fetch some from the creek. If he would not be otherwise needed, he would do his homework while it was still daylight. At night the family might turn on the kerosene lamp. After the evening meal, they would have family worship and tell stories until each felt like sleeping and would then go to bed.

Since the nights were cold, the fire in the middle of the house would be on and thick blankets would be covering the family. They might have put on warm clothes to have a more comfortable night. They would sleep in two different rooms—males and females separately. One room would be kept for visitors. His home could be a shelter to nine people—his mother and father, four brothers, and two sisters. Although the nights would be cold, father would insist on keeping the windows open as they need fresh air to breathe. Some nights he might join his friends to go hunting for cuscus or birds.

On Friday, he and his brothers might collect honey from trees or rocks. They would strain it and put it in a bucket or another container, then sweeten cassava, taro, banana, or tubers with delicious honey as a special Sabbath treat. However, if it was a school holiday or weekend, life was much more interesting. He would still do the regular chores—work in the garden, fetch firewood, and bring water, but other than that he would not be needed at home and he would spend all day with his friends. One of their favorite

Context

activities would be to go hunting with a catapult or bow and arrow they made or to prepare a *mumu* (explanation follows).

Making a *mumu* was a whole day adventure. They would dig a hole in the ground in which they would light a fire. Carefully chosen stones from the river, the white ones *(kombuglo bagle)*, would be heated in the fire until they were very hot. When the fire died out, they would cover the stones with ferns or banana leaves and then line up their *kaukau* (sweet potato), banana, some *kumu* (green leafy vegetables) on top of these. They would then cover it all with more banana leaves and wait and tell stories until the food was cooked, which could take several hours. Excitement would be in the air because the food would be just theirs; they prepared it themselves and could eat it by themselves. Of course, mother would prepare family dinner, which he would also enjoy. The family dinner might be the only meal of the day, and that would be all right. If there was food available at other times, that was even better.

If hunting or *mumu* was not the play of the day, perhaps playing marbles was. Some children would buy them, others would win them by playing well. While he would be playing with three to five other boys from his four-family village, his sisters would be perfecting their skills of making patterned *bilums* (stringed bags), or they would be preparing a *pitpit* (plant) mat for the floor. In a home where there was no electricity, no running water, no radio or television, and no telephone, another exciting day would finish with more bedtime stories shared and eagerly listened to by family members: stories about the day's activities or history of the ancestors of the *Gukbuk Naru* clan.

It could be one day in a three- to four-week period when he would get to eat his favorite food. This would be red pandanus or *komba* as they call it, a palm plant which could be red in colour (called *wo*), yellow (called *kigl-a-wa*), or orange (called *de-komba*). *Komba* is a seasonal plant and bears fruit once a year. It is naturally oily and tastes nice. It is so delicious that people boil it and cream it with vegetables like beans, broccoli, cabbage, lettuce, pumpkin tips, sago tips, banana, taro, and sweet potato. There is also wild pandanus, which is similar to red pandanus, but it is a type of nut

17

grown in the mountains. When wild pandanus season arrived the family would migrate to the forest with food, bedding, tools, and whatever else would be needed to survive those weeks away from the house. They would wait for pandanus nuts to fall on the ground. They would first let the rats take their share, since they believe that rats planted these trees. Then they would collect the rest of the nuts. Once back home, they would use wild pandanus in a barter system to exchange for red pandanus or sweet potato, or to give to distant friends who did not have wild pandanus.

Growing up in the highlands also seems to affect a person's body size. Ivo Mueller and Thomas A. Smith report that those from the highlands were found to be "heavier, those from mid-altitude regions shorter but heavier for their length than lowland children, children from areas with high relief of terrain were generally smaller while those from areas with high seasonality of rainfall and regular rainfall deficits were taller but lighter;"[18] however, "all factors connected with a higher socioeconomic status of a family were positively correlated with child growth."[19]

There are certain features which are specific to certain areas of PNG, and local people will know where a person comes from by looking at the shape of their nose. A Highlander will have an easily identified flat nose. Culturally, another feature by which a person is recognized is tattoos which are particular to an area.

It has been shown thus far that the place where a child grows up plays a significant part in the formation of their worldview. All these factors form part of the psychosocial development of that child. How that development is seen in Melanesia and the Western world will be explored in the next chapter.

---

18. Mueller and Smith, "Patterns," 105.
19. Ibid.

CHAPTER 2

Psychosocial Development

HUMAN BEINGS GROW AND change from conception until death. They develop physically, emotionally, cognitively, morally, spiritually, and socially. Each person is unique and grows and develops in a unique way, influenced by parents, society, and the environment. There are certain indicators of maturity that adults notice in a child and expect to see at certain ages. Some indicators are universal and apply to persons across the globe. For example, the menarche is a sign that a girl is becoming a woman, capable of reproduction. But the timing of the menarche in the life of a girl is not as universal, because it may range from ten to sixteen and a half years of age.[1] Some indicators are culture based. For example, in Australia a young woman cannot marry until she is legally an adult, eighteen years of age, although she has been menstruating regularly for several years (i.e., physically able to reproduce), while in another culture she would already have been married and had children.

Psychosocial development, as seen in Melanesia and the Western world, is the topic of this chapter. It is necessary to view and compare the two. PNG is influenced by both, as will be more clearly seen in the next chapter.

---

1. *Encyclopaedia Britannica*, 15th ed., s.v., "Human Growth and Development."

Part 1: Youth Ministry Challenge in PNG

Melanesian View of Psychosocial Development

In describing the Melanesian view of psychosocial development, it is important to declare from the outset that no universal view can be applied to all Melanesians. There are many cultures, contexts, and languages in Melanesia influencing social development in different ways in various environments. Views described in this chapter will be based on stories about growing up in PNG, either disclosed by indigenous residents or Western observers, census data, and research findings.

One of the earliest descriptions of the psychosocial development of children in PNG comes from Margaret Mead in her book *Growing Up in New Guinea: A Study of Adolescence and Sex in Primitive Societies*, originally published in 1930. "This account is the result of six months' concentrated and uninterrupted field work . . . in the centre of the Manus village of Peri."[2] It is specific to this particular village in a particular island in the particular year. She returned to Manus in 1964 to find "tremendous educational and political changes, and very few economic changes," and described those in a later book titled *New Lives for Old*.[3]

The newest publication dealing with the development of children in PNG, printed in 2009, is actually a collection of personal accounts of growing up in PNG written in the 1960s and 1970s, describing the childhood of the authors or stories their parents told them about their growing up.[4] There are other personal accounts that are helpful. Sir Paulias Matane, former Governor General of PNG, published memories of his childhood in 1972 as a story.[5] He talks about his birth, earliest years, his mother's death, and days of mourning. He describes life in a men's house, learning magic, his first pig hunt, and his primary and secondary schooling.

A number of available materials report specific details in the life of an adolescent, especially initiation rites. Gilbert Herdt

2. Mead, *Growing Up*, 15.
3. Ibid., 265.
4. Fenbury, *Childhood in Papua New Guinea*.
5. Matane, *My Childhood in New Guinea*.

collected some of them in *Rituals of Manhood: Male Initiation in Papua New Guinea*, where authors depict initiation rites in different areas of PNG.[6] Very helpful is Ann Chowning's article in the *Encyclopaedia of Papua New Guinea* on "Child Rearing and Socialization." The author looks at stages in the development of a child until it reaches adulthood. She also gives examples from various places in order to point out either general trends or extreme opposite customs. Chowning was able to make only a one-sentence generalization: "Everywhere, so far as we know, babies are normally suckled for more than a year and girls are expected to assume adult responsibilities much earlier than boys."[7] For her, important points in child rearing are early infancy, feeding, caring for the baby, appearance and adornment, walking, talking, toilet training, ceremonial in infancy, and weaning. When she looks at socialization, she looks at the attitudes towards education, social education, methods of education, play, sex in childhood, ceremonial in childhood, and achieving adulthood.

What is common in descriptions of child development from the early reports is that from the earliest age children are deliberately prepared for adulthood. Ian Hogbin noticed in 1946 in Wogeo that after weaning, children are "regarded as already in some degree a responsible being worthy of admission to a place in their own world," although they have ample opportunity for play.[8] This was evident by assigning part of a garden to the child, a couple of young pigs, their presence at dances taken for granted, and being carefully decorated. For him, "perhaps the most striking proof of the grown-ups' acceptance of the child as already one of them is provided by their frequent long-winded explanations" to the child although the child may not yet be able to understand the explanations.[9] However, he noticed that early teenagers hardly ever play during the day, as they are absorbed in adult concerns.

6. Herdt, *Rituals of Manhood*. Other works in this area include Allen, *Male Cults* and Maher, *New Men of Papua*.
7. Chowning, "Child Rearing," 156.
8. Hogbin, "New Guinea," 278.
9. Ibid., 279.

Part 1: Youth Ministry Challenge in PNG

In Melanesia, the youth population may be considered those of eleven to thirty years of age. They would consider themselves youth and would participate in youth programs.[10] The national census uses classification of cohorts zero to four, five to nine, ten to fourteen, fifteen to nineteen, and twenty to twenty-four years of age.[11] In her book *Childhood in Papua New Guinea: Personal Accounts of Growing Up in a Changing Society*, editor Helen Sheils Fenbury has divided the stages in development from birth and infancy, early childhood, middle childhood, and adolescence.[12] Patricia K. Townsend identified infants as those under age one, young children from ages one to six years, school-age children from seven to twelve, and youth those above twelve.[13] Some places differentiate developmental stages by the title their language uses for a person. In Dobuan community, five stages in the life of a person are identified (approximately): one to twelve years is the first phase, thirteen to sixteen the second, seventeen to twenty-four the third, twenty-five to forty-four the fourth, and over forty the fifth and final stage. Different names are given for males and females in each of these stages. Translated in English they would be male/female child, small young man/woman, young unmarried man/woman, becoming adult male/female, and old/big man/woman, respectively.[14]

The age of a child is not as important as the signs of development, since some children, even today, do not know their own age.[15] Various signs of development used to be acknowledged

10. Zocca and Groot, *Young Melanesian Project*, 5.

11. National Statistical Office of Papua New Guinea, accessed May 15, 2013, online: http://www.spc.int/prism/country/pg/Stats/About_NSO/about.htm.

12. This is how *Childhood in Papua New Guinea* is divided into sections on its contents page.

13. Townsend, *Situation*.

14. See David Duigu's chapter, "Growing Up in a Dobuan Society," in Fenbury, *Childhood*, 25.

15. In PNG, birth registry only happens in formal birthing places, like hospitals and clinics. Such facilities are not available in remote villages. Recently I met one young man who now lives with a family at PAU, who does not know how old he is—all of his immediate family died in tribal warfare, some of which he witnessed. His foster parents have assessed him to be around twelve years old.

Psychosocial Development

publicly in the society by performing ceremonies, dances, and feasts, but that is now only happening in remote rural areas. It is however important to make note of some such customs. In Barok society in New Ireland, "the child is not taken outdoors until he or she can hold his or her head up. . . . Supplementary feeding usually starts as the child's incisor teeth erupt."[16] Toilet training starts when a child is able to walk and run around and understands instructions. Parents and other relatives actively follow a child's physical development and expect psychosocial development to match the physical development. In Enga, "when a girl is two years old she could be dressed like a girl by her parents. She must always sit where women sit."[17] If a child is a boy, "from the age of two upwards he . . . must always sit where men sit, and soon sleep in the men's house. When visitors come . . . [he] must be polite, e.g. shake hands, fetch water for the visitor, not be greedy for food but ask if the visitor is satisfied."[18] Physical changes are also indicators of maturity. In Dobuan society, a male is considered adult when his chest is flattened and there is "the change in the features of the cheeks. In females, the main physical factor is the fall of the breasts. After these changes, which normally appear around the ages of nineteen to twenty-four years, they are regarded as matured people."[19]

From an early age the child's development is closely related to the roles he or she is expected to perform as an adult. The child learns to abide by the norms of conduct the society places on them. Parents, older siblings, and relatives make sure that children are taught all the skills they will need, whether it be how to grow or hunt for food, how to prepare tools, how to treat other people and property, or to be morally and socially acceptable in their village.

---

16. David Sangavalin Linge, "Barok Society, New Ireland, and Its Customs Surrounding Childbirth," in Fenbury, *Childhood*, 36–37.

17. Penjore Pilyo, "Sex and Sex-Roles, Fears, etc: Brief Reports: Early Childhood in an Enga Family," in Fenbury, *Childhood*, 58.

18. Ibid.

19. Duigu, "Growing Up," 27.

Part 1: Youth Ministry Challenge in PNG

When a child reaches puberty, initiation rites are performed. That applies to boys and girls, although the ceremonies are very different for each and done separately. For girls, they are usually performed at the onset of menarche but can also happen any time the parents may decide. In the Tufi area there are two such ceremonies for girls. The first one is when her age is "between eleven and twenty. Usually it is fifteen for this first ceremony, then eighteen for the second ceremony."[20] In the same society only one ceremony is performed for the boys, after which they are considered adults.

Initiation rites are very different in various parts of PNG. For females they are mostly very happy occasions, while for males they can be very painful. Some examples are ear and nose piercing, tattooing, circumcision, bloodletting from the penis, beating, scolding, and even anal penetration performed by older adults. They are all aimed at making a strong man and end in big community celebrations where he is accepted into society as a man, pride of the family. With Christianity now largely influencing the culture, such ceremonies have been abandoned and somewhat replaced by the celebration of baptism and graduation.

Traditionally, when a child is born, parents are delighted whether the child is a girl or a boy. A "perfect" family has an equal number of girls and boys born into it. However, gender starts to play a significant part in the child's life soon after birth. It is possible to have a certain role assigned to a male child in one part of the country, while the same role could be a female role in another part of the country.[21] Regardless, each child in its own society would know and abide by clearly defined gender roles. Mostly they are taught by parents. Fathers teach their sons, and mothers their daughters.

Education of children has always been important. It is part of the survival of an individual, but more importantly the survival of

---

20. Justin Abel Gevoya, "Ceremonies for Adolescents—Tufi Area, Northern (Oro) Province," in Fenbury, *Childhood*, 82.

21. "Whereas the Nakanai expect boys to be stoical and girls to be volatile, the Arapesh permit only boys to weep and indulge in fits of rage. The Wogeo and Siuai reproach girls for any display of violence, reserving such behaviour for boys, while the Sengseng teach baby girls to chase and beat boys in anticipation of the later courtship patterns." Chowning, "Child Rearing," 162.

Psychosocial Development

a clan and tribe, and as such, considered sacred. Parents are eager to teach and explain, while children are equally eager to learn. Imitation is the most common way of learning, but demonstration is given when the child displays an interest. Hogbin noticed that "the explanations are so detailed that the need for seeking additional information seldom arises, and 'why' questions, the everlasting bane of parents in our own [Western] community, are rarely heard."[22] By the time a child reaches late adolescence, he or she is able to perform all daily tasks. Nevertheless, even married young people recognize that they have much to learn, especially as the secrets of magic are not fully disclosed, and in the company of old people they are but children.[23]

The most comprehensive, more recent, research on youth was conducted in 1992 by the Melanesian Institute of Goroka. It was mandated by the churches who expressed that young people are "deeply affected by social changes" and were "increasingly alienated from the church's message and programs and at the same time increasingly alienated from their own culture, guidance of parents and traditional leaders."[24] The Young Melanesian Project (YMP) looked at issues pertaining to youth: education, marriage and family life, social problems, religion, livelihood, social order, and justice. The 1,630 young people who participated in the orally administered individual questionnaire commented that "it was a bit hard and not really a Melanesian way of doing things," but "finally, someone has understood us."[25]

Psychosocial development is affected by the changes in society, and emerging issues are different today compared to five years ago, even more so thirty or a hundred years ago. Jeline Giris and Teresia Rynkiewich point out domestic violence and HIV/AIDS as the two main issues affecting women and children in the PNG society today.[26] Both of these factors are serious threats to social

22. Hogbin, "New Guinea," 285.
23. Ibid., 163.
24. Zocca and Groot, *Young Melanesian Project*, preface.
25. Ibid.
26. Giris and Rynkiewich, "Emerging Issues," 1–30.

25

Part 1: Youth Ministry Challenge in PNG

stability and both are increasing in prevalence. They recognized that traditional ways still impact the society, but modern ways do as well. "Men and women no longer have to accept all the customs and ideas of the past as rules for behaviour or roles for men and women today. Customs of PNG evolved to fit the traditional village life; because we live differently now, we need to reconsider what we want, what we value and who we want to be."[27] Some of the answers will be found in understanding the roots and issues of modern Western life.

Western Stages of Psychosocial Development

The industrial revolution ushered in many changes to Western society. Although it was not the only influence, it greatly impacted families. Before the industrial revolution, most families were part of agrarian communities. Each member had a role and work to do. Relationships were well regulated by the society based on the physical growth and maturity of an individual. With different job opportunities increasing, fewer people needed to work the land, and more of them gravitated towards factories and industrial centers.

It could be argued that there used to be two stages in the development of a person: child and adult, with a brief interval between the two. Following the industrial revolution a third stage was noticed: that of adolescence, where a person is not a child anymore and not fully adult yet. Jeffrey J. Arnett states several other factors influencing the lengthening of the adolescent stage: "the enactment of laws restricting child labor, new requirements for children to attend secondary school, and the development of the field of adolescence as an area of scholarly study."[28]

G. Stanley Hall is considered "the founder of the scholarly study of adolescence."[29] His interest in adolescent development included their physical health, intellectual, emotional, moral,

27. Ibid., 27.
28. Arnett, *Adolescence*, 9. His comment reflects changes from 1890 to 1920, otherwise called the "Age of Adolescence."
29. Ibid., 11.

and social development, and adolescent love. His theories were based on little available data and more on the ideology of the time. Charles Darwin proposed the evolution theory with natural selection and survival of the fittest; Jean Lamarck espoused that acquired skills are passed on to new generations; Friedrich Nietzsche held that talented people could be selected for special training to pull the whole society toward excellence; Ernst Haeckel developed the recapitulation theory; and Hall proposed the theory of adolescence. It was a time of great "storm and stress," because it is a repetition of the struggles people went through as they separated from other species. But it was also a time for shaping a young person for excellence in order to bring about a new, improved generation of people. His theory was soon questioned and rejected, but the view of adolescence being a time of storm and stress is still debated one hundred years later and it seems rooted in popular thinking. One of the first persons who rejected Hall's universal theory of adolescence being a time of turmoil was Margaret Mead, who studied adolescence in "primitive societies." She published her observations of Samoans and [Papua] New Guineans where there was no stress associated with adolescence.[30]

Since Hall's ground-breaking theories, much research and publishing came to light.[31] Different areas of development were looked at: biological, cognitive, moral, social, religious, and personality, to name a few. Some scientists were not studying adolescents in particular, but their work impacts the understanding of adolescents.

Sigmund Freud developed his theories about personality by studying himself, by observing his patients and trying different methods to help them. He identified different levels of consciousness. He identified these levels as unconscious, preconscious and conscious and claimed that people are affected by their unconscious and preconscious although they are not aware of it. He found that the best way to release the tensions coming from the unconscious is by talking about past and present lives. His most popular work

30. Mead, *Growing Up* and *Coming of Age*.
31. See Senn et al., "Insights," 1–107.

is written for ordinary people, to explain why they tend to forget names and words and conceal memories and why they make mistakes in speech, reading, and writing.[32] Freud divided the mind into three structures: Id, a collection of basic instincts and drives that a person is born with; Ego, the conscious self; and Super Ego, the unconscious self that was developed through social interaction with the world. While trying to map the mind, he also accepted the view that the body creates psychic energy—libido—which is the innate force that motivates all thoughts, feelings, and behaviors.

Freud is perhaps best known for his view of psychosexual development. He proposed that bodily maturation brings about crises in life. This is due to sexual instincts that need to be brought under control. From stage to stage, the child's sexual instincts are expressed in different ways, and social pressures help him or her to control them. The first stage he named oral stage, which starts at birth and is expressed through sucking and swallowing. Other stages follow: anal, phallic stage, latency period, and finally genital stage. Genital stage starts with the development of genitalia at the onset of puberty and is complete at the end of adolescence, when a person is considered mature. That is, unless the child had traumas and unresolved issues. If so, then in adulthood, he or she would exhibit similar kinds of behaviors associated with the stage of psychosexual development in which unresolved issues occurred. Freud saw the early years of child development of crucial importance to the well-being of an adult person.

Freud's ideas strongly influenced scientists throughout the twentieth century, particularly Carl Jung, Alfred Adler, and Erik Erikson. Each of these first followed Freud, but then moved away from his theories or developed their own based on his. Erikson saw that people grow and mature throughout their lives and do not stop that process after adolescence. Erikson's eight developmental stages are in some way related to Freud's but are based on a very different foundation. For Erikson, they are tests of character which if positively resolved eventually form a mature person. The two opposing tendencies in developmental stages are trust versus

32. Freud, *Psychopathology*.

Psychosocial Development

mistrust, autonomy versus shame, initiative versus guilt, industry versus inferiority, identity versus role confusion, intimacy versus isolation, generativity versus stagnation, and integrity versus despair.[33] Those in puberty and adolescence face a crisis of identity they need to solve by deciding who they want to become. Their mind is "essentially a mind of the *moratorium*, a psychosocial stage between childhood and adulthood, and between the morality learned by the child, and the ethics to be developed by the adult."[34]

Jean Piaget researched the areas of child play, dreams, imitation, and the child's conception of numbers. He tried to discover the origins of intelligence in children; the moral judgment of the child; and the child's conception of the world. He looked at the growth of logical thinking from childhood to adolescence. He proposed four stages of cognitive development occurring at certain ages of a child.[35] The sensory-motor period which he divided into six parts starts with the reflex activity of a newborn and ends when the child is around two years old and starts to think. The pre-operational stage lasts from the second to seventh year, the stage of concrete operations from about seven until twelve, to finally reach the stage of formal operation. Through these stages a child moves from concrete to abstract thinking, where they can solve problems in their minds. Piaget's stage theory can be seen as an "attempt to explain 'why' children develop as they do."[36]

Lawrence Kohlberg was concerned with moral development and suggested that there are three levels of moral reasoning. Preconventional reasoning is when morally correct decisions are made in view of possible punishment or reward accompanying such decision. The conventional level is reached when socially approved values and standards are internalised and acted out—at ten to thirteen years of age. The third level is the postconventional level, where an individual is acting in a morally right way according to the universal

---

33. Erikson, *Childhood*, 247–69, especially the chapter titled "Eight Ages of Man."
34. Ibid., 262–63.
35. See Piaget, *Origins*.
36. McConnell, *Understanding*, 497.

principles of justice that he or she personally committed to uphold, regardless whether they are socially acceptable or not. This level is reached between fifteen to nineteen years of age. Early adolescents, according to Kohlberg, are starting to behave from internalized socially approved values, and late adolescents base their moral decisions on universal principles they want to live by. Changes in stages of moral development, however, do not come only by age and maturation. Cognitive skills and social influences also affect one's moral reasoning. Adolescents need to come to terms with who they are—resolving their identity crisis—before they can commit to moral values of the highest order which go beyond what is socially accepted, but truly right. Chap Clark has possibly identified a new phase of adolescent development for midadolescents who lack the ability "to see contradictions as contradictions and the ability to easily rationalize seemingly irreconcilable beliefs, attitudes, or values" and have developed a "world beneath" in which they live. Perhaps of more serious concern for him is that "adolescents have been abandoned" by "the adults who have the power and experience to escort them into the greater society."[37]

There is no consensus among scholars on the terminology or age of youth. According to Hall at the beginning of the twentieth century, youth or preadolescence is between ages eight and twelve, while adolescence is from the age of twelve till twenty-four.[38] At the turn of the twenty-first century, Kenda Creasy Dean, Chap Clark, and David Rahn divided adolescence into three sections: early (eleven to thirteen), middle (fourteen to nineteen), and late (nineteen till mid-twenties).[39] Arnett calls the last category "emerging adulthood."[40] Although such divisions were seen earlier, the age assigned to each is different. In 1975, Hershel D. Thornburg assigned seventeen to nineteen years to late adolescence, while for Dean, Clark, and Rahn, late adolescence is from nineteen

37. Clark, *Hurt*, 21.
38. In Berzonsky, *Adolescent Development*, 33.
39. Dean et al., *Starting Right*, 50.
40. Arnett puts the age for emerging adulthood "roughly from 18 to 25" (*Adolescence*, 4).

until mid-twenties.⁴¹ Even as late as 1981, Michael D. Berzonsky divided adolescence into two stages: early and late.⁴²

It appears that there is a widening gap between physical maturation of a person and entry into adulthood. There is general agreement among scholars that currently children mature physically earlier than they used to. A firm indicator is the age of menarche in girls. In Norway, in the 1840s the average age was seventeen years, while in the 1980s it was thirteen. In the United States, "the average age of menarche has been declining an average of about four months per decade for the past century."⁴³

Much more difficult to ascertain is when a person ceases to be an adolescent and becomes an adult, and what the indicators would be that such a transition has actually taken place. In pre-industrial societies there were rites of passage which marked entry into the adult world. In today's complex world, such clear demarcations do not exist. Governments pass laws to make certain that young people are allowed adult privileges when they reach a certain age. For example, in Australia, at the age of eighteen, a person can legally purchase alcohol, get married, get a driver's licence, join the army, and vote. Just because they are allowed, it does not mean that all eighteen-year-olds will purchase alcohol, get married, get a driver's licence, join the army, and vote. These laws will not define whether they are now adults, whether they see themselves as adults or whether society accepts them as adults.

Since Hall's initial studies on adolescents, much scientific study of adolescents has been conducted. The main ways of conducting studies were through questionnaires, interviews, ethnographic research, biological measurement, experimental research, and more recently, daily records. The results from studies are usually written, peer reviewed, and published in journals such as *Journal of Adolescent Research*, *Youth & Society*, *Journal of Youth & Adolescence*, and *Journal of Research on Adolescence*.

---

41. Thornburg, *Development*, 5.
42. Berzonsky, *Adolescent Development*, 3.
43. Santrock, *Adolescence*, 81.

Part 1: Youth Ministry Challenge in PNG

Much can be learned about youth from research in other areas—psychology, education, anthropology, sociology, and religion. Today, adolescence is a separate field of study.[44] It involves biological and cognitive development of an individual, but also looks at the contexts of adolescent development: families, peers, schools, and culture. With studies of adolescents, researchers attempt to find out more about social, emotional, and personality development as seen in self-identity, gender, sexuality, moral development, values, religion, achievement, careers, and work.

No textbook on adolescents can be found anymore that does not assess adolescent problems. The problems adolescents face are related to substance use, juvenile delinquency, depression and suicide, eating disorders, and stress. They are "growing up too fast too soon" and are then "all grown up and no place to go."[45] Substance use is a term used for the problem of using alcohol, cigarettes, and illegal drugs, such as marijuana, LSD, cocaine, and ecstasy. Scientists try to identify current and past rates of substance use to see the trends. The best source for such data in the United States is the Monitoring the Future studies. They found that alcohol use is common, and cigarettes the next most common substance used during adolescence.[46] Such studies also show which segment of society has the highest prevalence. In the United States it was found that Native Americans have the highest drug use, followed by Hispanic youth, and black and Asian youth the lowest. However, race is certainly not the only influencing factor. John M. Wallace Jr. and Jerald G. Bachman argue that "several lifestyle factors—including educational values and behaviors, religious commitment, and time spent in peer-oriented activities—strongly relate to drug use and help to explain subgroup

---

44. The number of journals reporting on research about adolescents and adolescence, and the number of textbooks in this field are clear indications that adolescence is a separate field of study.

45. These are titles of two books by David Elkind: *All Grown Up & No Place to Go* and *Hurried Child: Growing Up Too Fast Too Soon*.

46. Wallace and Bachman, "Explaining," 333–57.

differences."[47] The most affected age group with this problem is emerging adults who are college students.

Today it is not only scientific studies that examine youth issues. Media plays a significant role as well. Jason Sternberg finds "one of the most disturbing signs in the news media's treatment of young people is the increasingly negative coverage . . . and the potential impact this has, not only on the way older generations view youth, but on how young people view themselves."[48] It is to the media and other influences on the youth in PNG that this book turns next in order to clearly hear the biblical call of adoption.

---

47. Ibid., 333.
48. Sternberg, "Young," 34.

CHAPTER 3

Influences and Ecology

THERE ARE POWERS THAT affect a person, sometimes without any effort on their part. Whether a person is aware of it or not, relationships are formed between human groups and their physical environment. These are called influences and ecology. In order to help clarify the youth ministry challenge in PNG, media, family, and animism are discussed as the three main influences for a young person in PNG, and their relationship with that environment will be acknowledged.

Media

Technological revolution is impacting PNG. Its spread is great, and yet not wide enough to match the standards in the developed world. For example, communication explosion through mobile phones has been dramatic in the past few years. In 2002, there were no mobile phones in PNG. When B-Mobile was introduced in 2003, it was possible to see a few people trying to find reception spots, especially at the outskirts of the cities. Even today, B-Mobile does not have a good coverage country wide. It was only when competition, Digicel, was allowed in 2007, that the use of mobile

Influences and Ecology

phones skyrocketed.¹ Although it seems that everybody in the cities has a mobile phone, this is not a fact.

Disparity between those who have access to information and communication technology infrastructure and services in PNG is far greater for those living in rural areas. On average, "access to telephone services is not widely available; combined fixed-line and mobile-cellular teledensity is six per one hundred persons."² For those who do have access, more user options of use are available apart from calling another person.³ The following paragraphs will describe media as radio, television, internet and print, and its influence on the youth of PNG.

Radio

There are several radio stations that can be heard in PNG. Some of those are localized and cater to the city population, while others are broadcast nation wide. In Port Moresby, several radio stations are available. Two are Christian: FM Light and 2G FM, a community radio station broadcasting from Pacific Adventist University. One of the most popular secular stations is Nau FM on 96.5 FM, and it is aimed at a younger audience. Nau FM broadcasts in English and plays Western music (i.e., mainly from the United States and Australia), which makes this station very popular for the younger generation. Yumi FM broadcasts in Tok Pisin and is intended for an older audience, but is also operated by Nau FM.⁴

    1. "Telecommunications," in AusAID, *Pacific Economic Survey 2008*, 43–46. See also Webb, *Assessment*, 8.

    2. "Oceania—Papua New Guinea—Media," *Nationmaster.com*, accessed September 16, 2010, online: http://www.nationmaster.com/red/country/pp-papua-new-guinea/med-media&all=1.

    3. NASFUND sent out an e-newsletter titled "A First for Superannuation and Savings & Loan in PNG!" on September 17, 2010, announcing access to svings and loans and superannuation balances through a mobile phone facility. Features already available include sending credit to another person's mobile phone and purchasing electricity units for one's dwelling.

    4. "Radio Station World: Papua New Guinea," Radiostationworld.com, accessed July 23, 2009, online: http://radiostationworld.com/locations/Papua_New_ Guinea/.

Part 1: Youth Ministry Challenge in PNG

Yumi FM plays mostly local music, something which older audiences appreciate. Another example of a localized radio service is CDI FM, a community radio station located in Kikori Training Centre. "It supports the work of CDI Foundation by broadcasting information related to health, education, agriculture and general rural community development to communities in Kikori."[5]

Karai Radio, operated by National Broadcasting Commission (NBC), covers all of PNG through the FM frequency in the National Capital District, while AM and SW services take the programs to every village.[6] Radio Australia and BBC World Service Asia/Pacific, Paradise FM, and Catholic Radio Network are a few other radio services providing news, music, stories, and religious topics.

There are regional radio networks, like Radio Kundu AM that has fourteen provincial stations nationwide, operated by NBC-PNG.[7] These radio networks are very important "because one can have a radio running on batteries even in the bush. Messages are spread mainly via radio. There are regular information programs where deaths, appointments, and other newsworthy items are announced."[8]

Small radio receivers are easily acquired, making this media readily accessible. Every shop that plays music is tuned into one of the available local stations. Office workers often listen to a radio station at work. They like to interact with the radio presenters by phoning in questions or answers to questions which the station posed, and they send greetings to each other, birthday wishes to relatives, and request special music.

Some mobile phones and media-playing devices have access to radio programs. Those who can use Internet can also listen to some local radio stations through this media and even more so to

---

5. Ibid.

6. "TV and Radio Channels Papua New Guinea," accessed September 19, 2010, online: http://www.ostamyy.com/TV-radio-channels /Papua-New-Guinea.htm.

7. "Radio Station World: Papua New Guinea."

8. Leh and Kennedy, "Instructional," 98.

Influences and Ecology

the radio stations around the world.[9] With all these devices growing in popularity and availability, radio is ever more accessible and it is in fact "the most-used medium."[10]

Television

The first television broadcast came to PNG in July 1987, with the EM TV station. It is still the main free-to-air television station. Although "by 2002 the station operated two transmitters in Port Moresby and six others around the country, [it was] reaching just under two million people."[11] EM TV broadcasts local news, shows, and selected programs from Australia mostly in the evenings. During the day, the station sometimes transmits very basic locally made educational programs.[12] The company is owned by Fiji TV under the name Media Niugini Limited. Today EM TV is "received in real time via satellite in thirty-eight centres throughout Papua New Guinea." This is "approximately 45 percent of PNG's total population."[13] However, even though this percent of the population can receive a signal from EM TV, it is still very difficult to ascertain the exact number of patrons.[14] According to Asian Development Bank's statistical report, only 10 percent of the population has a television set.[15]

In 2008, a new free-to-air channel, NTS, that is trading as Kundu 2, was launched as the state-run National Television

---

9. "Papua New Guinea Radio Stations," Tunein.com, accessed May 15, 2013, online: http://tunein.com/radio/Papua-New-Guinea-r100394/.

10. Leh and Kennedy, "Instructional," 98.

11. Tindall, "Papua New Guinea."

12. The official website of EM TV is http://www.emtv.com.pg. TV guide, weekly programs, and other information are available on this website.

13. "About Us," EMTV.com, accessed May 15, 2013, online: http://www.emtv.com.pg/about-us.

14. Lahari, "Challenges."

15. "ICT Indicators for Papua New Guinea," *Asian Development Bank* (ADB.org), accessed September 16, 2010, online, http://www.adb.org/ICT/png-indicators.asp.

Part 1: Youth Ministry Challenge in PNG

Service. However, for those living in Port Moresby, and who can afford it, there is Hitron Internet, a television and radio provider with 117 television channels from all around the world, including fifteen stereo radio channels.

It can be argued that the majority of PNG children grow up in rural areas where there may be no electricity, no running water, no television, and no phone, but who are surrounded by nature; children who learn to work in the gardens for survival. There is a minority, however, who grow up in the cities where they have electricity, running water, and phones, but no garden. They also have access to the world outside PNG through television, especially those who have Hitron connection. The gap between the two groups is growing, even though the government is trying to provide access to over 420,000 Papua New Guineans in the provinces of Chimbu and East Sepik by 2015.[16]

Conversations with children in urban areas indicate they are in touch with all the latest movies and have strong opinions on which programs they like and dislike. They spend various lengths of time in front of the television either in their own homes or at friends' houses. Some have indicated that their television stays turned on all day although they may not be watching it all the time. When these children visit their relatives in the villages, they have little in common, but much to learn from each other.

Local shops offer many pirated DVDs with movies from around the world, increasingly from the Philippines and India. These can be watched on television sets with DVD players or on computers. Research in this area is needed to reveal more objective data regarding the use of television to find out not only how many Papua New Guineans have access to it, but also what kind of influence it has on those who do watch it.

---

16. "Improving Telecommunications Access in PNG's Rural Communities: Rural Communications Project," News & Broadcast, *World Bank*, accessed September 16, 2010, online: http://www.worldbank.org/en/country/png.

Internet

It was March 12, 1997, that Internet came to PNG. Today there are about five Internet service providers (ISP) in the country, all owned by foreign companies.[17] A few months after the introduction of the Internet to the country, the first website was launched by the University of Papua New Guinea. Today there are numerous websites promoting business and tourism and providing services. Following are a few examples.

Air Niugini is the main airline of PNG. Today information about all flights, national and international, are posted on their webpage. Regular features available from its site are purchasing tickets online, links with PNG Tourism, Visa information, and a currency converter. None of this was available until the end of 2006. The website has since had several upgrades.[18]

To purchase electricity or a mobile phone recharge card for either of the country's providers, Telikom or Digicel, a person has to go to a place where they are sold. In case the electricity credit runs out when the shop is closed, one would need to wait until the shop opens again, during which time goods in the fridge would be spoiled. Now there is a website on which this can be done from the comfort of the home. It is called Esishop. Although the initial set-up is somewhat cumbersome, once completed, a person only needs a credit card and internet access.

Many businesses, schools, universities, religious organizations, and associations, as well as the government of PNG, have websites. One wonders who the beneficiaries of these websites are in a country that has 6.4 computers per one hundred people and 1.8 Internet users per one hundred people.[19] Those who can afford this technology are people living in the major centers with well-paying jobs, not in the villages where over 80 percent of the

---

17. Kwasam, *Internet*.

18. "Air Niugini—Timeline," accessed September 20, 2010, online: http://www.michie.net/balus/pxtimeline.html.

19. "ICT Indicators," ADB.org, n.p.

Part 1: Youth Ministry Challenge in PNG

population lives. University students are some of the privileged ones, as most universities provide at least some Internet access.

Pacific Adventist University is a case in point, where the student-to-computer ratio is less than one to three, where computers are available also in the dormitories, and for those who have personal laptops, wireless Internet is available in several hotspots throughout the campus. The University is part of the PNGARNet (Papua New Guinea Academic and Research Network) together with five other universities and two research institutes in the country and has access to the Internet through satellite connection bypassing local ISP providers. Students have free access to search engines like JSTOR, ProQuest, SAGE Online Journals, ATLA/ATLAS, Hinari, and others. They like to use e-mail and Internet for social purposes, thus access to Facebook and other social networks is restricted to night hours. Some have discovered, and been trapped with, the negative side of the Internet—pornography—but the University has policies in place to help those students. Students who have completed their studies tend to continue using the Internet when possible. Some will use social networks like Facebook, others will keep in touch with lecturers and friends through web-based e-mail, which they can access once they are in a town center with an Internet café or through a friend who has Internet access, if they do not have it. Internet connection is also possible through mobile phones, although it is quite costly and very slow at this point in time.

Print

There are two daily newspapers in PNG, the *National* and the *Post Courier*. Both are in English. Their circulation in centers other than the Port Moresby area is limited, with fifteen copies per one thousand people.[20] Two weekly newspapers are *Wantok Niuspepa*, published in Tok Pisin, and *The Independent*, published in English. Selected articles from these four newspapers, except *Wantok*

---

20. Tindall, "Papua New Guinea," n.p.

Influences and Ecology

Niuspepa, are also available on the Internet on their respective sites. They are available to purchase from street vendors, grocery supermarkets, and stationary shops. The price for an issue will differ for people living in Port Moresby and those in other areas. *Post Courier* costs one kina in Port Moresby while it is one kina and fifty toea in other centers. The price difference is due to transport costs, as these papers are printed in Port Moresby and need to be transported to any other part of the country by plane.

Another English language newspaper, *Eastern Star*, is published in the city of Alotau every two weeks. Government news is printed once a month in *Hiri Nius*, with a circulation of five thousand, in the three main languages of the nation—English, Tok Pisin and Hiri Motu.[21] There are other publications also available for readers. *Post Courier* publishes a free monthly NAW magazine (*Newagewoman*) for its female readership. These are inserted into the regular *Post Courier*. *Rage* magazine is also available for those interested in entertainment, especially the music scene of PNG.

Both major daily newspapers have regional editions that are printed on a weekly basis. *The National* has *Highlands This Week*, *Lae News*, *Papua This Week*, and others, while the *Post Courier* has *Highlands Post*, *Islands Post*, and *Momase Post*.

Many Papua New Guineans have authored and published journal articles, books, and other publications. Particularly noteworthy is Sir Paulias Matane, former Governor General of PNG, who has published over thirty books and is planning to continue his publishing career. The latest one, prepared and published in collaboration with M. L. Ahuja, is *Papua New Guinea: Land of Natural Beauty and Cultural Diversity*.[22] Many of his books are journals of his many travels in the world, but he also encapsulates life in PNG, and as such has left a legacy to future generations.

Written expression, though, is not part of the PNG cultural make up because it is mainly an oral culture. Much of that culture can easily be lost if not written down. Languages are lost when

21. Ibid.

22. Matane and Ahuja, *Papua New Guinea*, lists 34 other books by Sir Paulias Matane.

the populations of villages decline. Knowledge about the way of life, including traditions, dress, medicinal plants, tool making, food preparation, songs, and dances can all be lost if not recorded. Many books about PNG have been written by foreigners. They are biased by the perspective or interpretation of reality which foreigners bring, regardless of how long they may have been in the country. Local writing, recording, and publishing should be encouraged. The National Research Institute and the Melanesian Institute are some of the entities in the country currently encouraging local literature.

At the same time, literacy in PNG is among the lowest in the world, estimated at 57.3 percent of the population.[23] Many cannot read or write and cannot even sign their name, the situation being worse for females. The *National Youth Policy* of 2007 set up a target to increase literacy by 10 percent by 2011, particularly for girls. According to the 2000 census, 33 percent of youth age twelve to twenty-five never attended school. Altogether 484,436 never attended school, of which 253,226 were females; 22,000 less than males.[24]

Family

In a conversation about family, it will soon be discovered that the definition of family is father, mother, and their children.[25] However, when prompted further, single-parent families and couples without children will also be considered family, albeit not desirable or approved by the community. Couples without children are assumed unhappy and traditional adoption practices are in place to address this need. The main reason for marriage is to have children to take care of parents and the necessary work at home and eventually to replace the parents.

For the sake of clarity, a look at the immediate family and the extended family is needed, although the boundaries between the

23. Commonwealth Secretariat, *Small States*, 139.
24. *National Youth Policy*, 36, 18.
25. In the course Health and Family, taught to mostly theology students at Pacific Adventist University, the definition of family is a perennial question.

two are not clearly defined. For example, when a man introduces his brother, he does not necessarily mean a brother from the same mother and father. A brother can mean a cousin, a stepbrother—sharing the same father or mother—a person adopted into the family, or even a person of the same faith. Someone who wants to know the exact family connectedness will have to ask additional questions for clarification.

Immediate and Extended Family

For an ordinary person, the ideal immediate family consists of father, mother, and children, preferably more than one. However, polygamy is still present in PNG. Some students at Pacific Adventist University have a biological mother, as well as a social mother or mothers, and brothers and sisters from a different mother but the same father. Anne Dickson-Waiko noted that "traditionally polygamy was commensurate with power and status, of being a 'bigman.'"[26] So it was a man who chose to have more than one wife in order to show his status and power. Today women also want power, and from that perspective would enter into marriage with a politician, for example, as his second or third wife.[27] Some men have one wife in the village to take care of business there and another one in town for show-off, or to take care of the business in town. There is a debate going on whether to abolish this practice or uphold it. Dickson-Waiko, in her article, replies to an earlier article written in favor of polygamy in PNG and disagrees with its author.

Today the preferred way of getting married is still through arranged marriages. Parents, uncles, and extended families decide who will marry whom, sometimes "without any knowledge or discussion with the girl."[28] Sometimes the arranged marriages are an exchange between the families: a young woman from one family or clan will marry a young man from another family or a clan, and

26. Dickson-Waiko, "Polygamy," 64.
27. Ibid.
28. Griffen, "Gender," 17.

Part 1: Youth Ministry Challenge in PNG

then the same would be reciprocated. Even in urban settings where it is more common to have the adolescents choose their marriage partners, an approval is sought from the elders of the family before marriage can take place. Those who decide to elope face difficulties in their community.

Bride price accompanying arranged marriage is also a common practice in PNG and the Pacific. Bride price is the exchange of goods for the bride. The goods that are exchanged have in time altered due to the introduction of money and other imported and technological goods. These exchanges happen both in rural and urban settings. Traditionally, and still today, shell money is given together with food items. Sadly, "in Port Moresby, for example, urbanites jokingly refer to young women as 'Toyotas,' since that is what their families will demand from prospective suitors."[29]

One of my students was extremely happy when his wife gave birth to a girl. They already had four sons but a daughter was very special. What made her more special was the bride price he would receive when she married. He owed much to his family who put their resources together in order to afford his wife. While having only sons, he could not return what he owed, but with the girl child, he would.[30]

The immediate family is usually graced with several siblings. In 2005, the total fertility rate for the female population was 3.8, which was a decrease of 0.6 from 2001.[31] Especially in the cities, where more family planning opportunities exist, where conditions for raising children exist, and where people are more educated, the trend to have fewer children is clear by simply looking at nearby families, church members, and acquaintances and comparing that with the generation before. The number of siblings in a family would have been between five and ten. A family with polygamous marriage would have more children still.

---

29. Rapaport, *Pacific Islands*, 201–2.

30. From a conversation with Robinson Diosi, a student from the Solomon Islands, in 2007. Although he is not a Papua New Guinean, for the practical purposes of this example, he might have been.

31. Commonwealth Secretariat, *Small States*, 147.

Influences and Ecology

Extended family plays a significant role in a person's life in PNG. Extended families often visit each other and that requires generous hospitality and is freely given out of respect for family ties. Extended families also rely on each other in difficult times. Berit Gustafsson says that "someone who might not have food in the house could always feel free to go to the house of his or her parents, a brother, a sister, an aunt, or other close kin. Should the demand include larger items or support, rarely would the demand be denied."[32]

This cooperation between extended families extends to issues of childbearing and provides adequate support. Adoption of children is a very common practice in PNG. Some time ago, I was talking with one lady on campus who told me that the next day she would receive a one-month-old baby girl. She continued to explain that this baby girl was coming from her husband's family. The mother of the child felt that she could not take care of the girl and looked for the nearest family member to give the child to.

Only a few days later I spoke to this lady again to make sure I understood the reason for the adoption of this girl and to inquire how things were going with the new family member. The reply was that the baby girl was still with her mother and would not come to live with them after all. The mother had since changed her mind, and perhaps found somebody to help with the care of the baby girl. My friend was relieved that she did not need to take care of this baby, but would have willingly and happily done so if needed.[33]

This story illustrates several things: adoption of children is common, it is practiced mostly among family members, it is quite simple—an arrangement between the families is enough—and it is revocable. Adoption of children can happen at any time in the life of a child and it is "facilitated by cultural beliefs that nurture—not just nature—creates kinship."[34]

---

32. Gustafsson, "Poverty," 16.

33. Benita Pano, conversation with author, August 10 and 12, 2008 (used by permission).

34. Rapaport, *Pacific Islands*, 199.

Part 1: Youth Ministry Challenge in PNG

The reasons for adoption vary. Most common is death of a parent, especially the mother.[35] When one couple in a family cannot have children, some close relative will give them their child or children. In some societies it is common to exchange children of siblings so their children feel more closely related and so that they will not intermarry.[36] Adoption also happens in order to keep land in the lineage,[37] or "to distribute people over sometimes limited landscapes."[38] It appears that "in the 'extended family' cultures of the Pacific most of them do not seem to worry about it."[39] This would need to be further researched. One of my students realized that he was adopted only in his late thirties and this information had shaken him at the time.

Discipline of children is a task shared among the community and extended family. It is not the sole duty of the parents. This is especially so in a village setting. Children are taught obedience and respect for adults, often in a very authoritarian way that does not allow children to express themselves, nor explain their situation. But in today's environment such practices often produce the opposite effect to the one desired. Particularly in the cities, it is possible to form firmer bonds with peers than with parents. Risky behavior often results because of peer pressure. When this becomes obvious to parents they tend to punish the child, which only makes the child even more fearful of parents, and the "opportunities for parental guidance" are reduced.[40] When this "commonly accepted Pacific practice of disciplining children with physical force" is addressed, "Pacific parents and community leaders will often vehemently defend the right to use physical punishment as

---

35. The maternal mortality ratio per 100,000 live births in PNG was 300 in the year 2000, while a UNESCO report estimates that number to have been 470 in 2005. WHO, "Maternal Mortality," 28.

36. Brady, *Transactions*, 100–101.

37. Epstein, *Gunantuna*, 70.

38. Rapaport, *Pacific Islands*, 199.

39. Townend, *One Plus One*, 43.

40 *State of Pacific Youth*, 32.

'part of our culture.'"[41] This may well be part of the extended family involvement.

Wantok System

Wantok is a term often used and widely accepted in PNG. The literal translation would be "one talk" which means "a person who speaks the same language." However, that translation does not explain the meaning behind the term. Students who come to my office sometimes say "I need to see my *wantoks* in town to find some help for fees." Or if there is a public holiday coming, they might say, "I'm going to stay with my *wantoks*." The meaning of *wantok* here could be understood as "relatives." But *wantok* means even more than that.

Wantok is a system of interrelationships within the clan or cultural group. *Wantoks* do also speak the same language. This is an important commonality in a country where over eight hundred languages are spoken. They come from the same village or area. Often they are blood relations—cousins, uncles, and aunties. They "stick together, sharing mutual respect, trust and desires for meaningful relationships and a sense of belonging."[42] That is how a student can go to town to find his *wantoks* and get some money from them to pay their fees. It is expected that *wantoks* will do that for each other. The "system becomes an insurance policy and a security system creating open dialogue obligating the other for return favour when the need arises."[43]

In a village setting, not the whole village would be *wantoks*. "Cooperation was confined to members of a clan, or a subclan, and only involved a fraction of a language group."[44] On the other hand, in the urban setting there is a different dimension to it.

---

41. Griffen, "Gender," 9.
42. Misha, "Case Study," 47.
43. Ibid.
44. Gustafsson, "Poverty," 12.

Part 1: Youth Ministry Challenge in PNG

It appears that "the further from home one goes the wider he is willing to extend his boundaries of *wantoks*."[45] *Wantoks* can be persons who share a common language, kinship, place, or area of origin, but also social or religious associations. This system operates in all aspects of modern life: "finding accommodation and a job, forming sports organisations, defending assaulted friends ('wantoks'), retaliating victims of fight and car accidents, forming small business enterprises, trying to gain prestige and political influence, etc."[46] It is deeply rooted in reciprocity in a positive sense where people can count on each other for help if need be.

This system can, however, be taxing on families. Regardless of a family's financial situation, if a *wantok* comes for a visit, they are obligated to be very hospitable and to do everything in their power to provide help or comfort. One student shared with me how he is perfectly free to go to his uncle to ask him to buy him a plane ticket to travel to the place he needs to go to. His uncle then would also be perfectly free to ask him for a similar favor at some other time and he would have to oblige, even if this means borrowing from others.

We could possibly use the term kinship to translate *wantok*. Kinship, then, needs to be understood as follows:

> Kin relations structure most islanders' everyday lives. Residence groups are based on kinship. Kinship determines the membership of many economic enterprises as well as political and religious associations. Most people live, work, politic, and worship with kin, and these relations define much of who they are. The extended family is common throughout the region, except among the most cosmopolitan.[47]

The sense of obligation is very strong, and goes beyond Western understanding of honesty and morality. Kin expectations can be very high. Some time ago I was talking with a business man from town, an expatriate, and he told me that one of his employees needed to take care of a hundred of his relatives in the village, not

---

45. Shaw, "Wantok," 194.
46. Janssen, "Wantoks," 289.
47. Rapaport, *Pacific Islands*, 198.

Influences and Ecology

only his family but his in-laws, too. When the person with income is a politician, the stakes are much higher, and loyalty to his *wantoks* is often termed "corruption."

For a Papua New Guinean living in the United States, *wantok* is anybody who comes from PNG, regardless of whether they are related or not, whether they speak the same language or not, whether they are from the same province or not. In this sense this term can be understood very broadly. It is also open to include foreigners. Foreigners who live in the country, who learn to speak the language, and who adopt the basic values of *wantokism* reciprocity are also considered *wantoks*. For example this reciprocity is between parents and children. Parents provide for their children and when the children grow up they provide for their parents, especially when the parents cannot look after themselves any more. Although *wantok* can be a neighbor, classmate, friend, or coworker, it is really the closest of kin that one can rely on if in trouble. So, a classmate will share food on occasion but it is the *wantok* that will provide real assistance if one is in serious trouble or for extended periods of time. A single person without a job may go from one relative to the other but if that person is not actively looking for job, and is not giving something in return, may find that *wantoks* will stop giving. Reciprocity is a requirement and if it becomes one sided it will cease.

Animism

A search for the meaning of the term "animism" will yield varying results. According to Ennio Mantovani, animism is "belief in personalized spiritual beings, such as souls, ghosts and spirits."[48] The *Merriam-Webster* dictionary explains it as "attribution of conscious life to objects in [nature] and phenomena of nature or to inanimate objects."[49] The recent *New Lion Handbook: The World's Religions*

---

48. Mantovani, *Introduction*, xi.

49. Two other definitions by Merriam-Webster are: "2: a doctrine that the vital principle of organic development is immaterial spirit" and "3: belief in the existence of spirits separable from bodies." *Merriam-Webster Online*, s.v.

Part 1: Youth Ministry Challenge in PNG

uses the term "primal religions" and "indigenous religions."[50] The meaning of "primal religions," applicable to what this section will call "animism" in the PNG setting, is defined as "religious systems of tribal groups having no literary tradition. They are characterized by a belief in various spiritual forces behind natural phenomena, a reverence for ancestors and a tight-knit social system which is sanctioned and held in being by the power of common myths."[51] While visiting a waterfall, two of the theology students showed me a curvy vine saying that in their animistic worldview this vine was very significant. It has special "powers," just like the waterfall itself, the stones, and other trees around it. But this belief goes further to include sorcery, witchcraft, and magic, the means to manipulate spirits for humanity's survival.

The animistic worldview is still prevalent in PNG today. This is perhaps because "Melanesians rely primarily on religious knowledge as their basis for knowing and understanding the world in which they live."[52] It is an integrated system where all of life's experiences are based on religious knowledge. While practicing magic and benevolent or malicious sorcery, "most of these tribal people would still claim to be Christians."[53] Kent Mundhenk notes that even after living with the tribe as a missionary for ten years, "very few were actually trusting in Christ alone for their salvation."[54]

Dale Goodson has lived with the Dowa tribe for ten years trying to understand their worldview. He found that in their worldview, "man manipulates or controls spiritual powers to accommodate his comfort and wishes. He does so through a

---

"animism," accessed September 26, 2010, online: http://www.merriam-webster.com/dictionary/animism.

50. Beaver et al., *Lion Handbook*, 413, 440. Partridge, *New Lion Handbook*, 457, 466. The term "primal religions" was used in the 1982 edition that by 2005 was changed again to "indigenous religions."

51. Beaver et al., *Lion Handbook*, 440.

52. Whiteman, "Melanesian Religions," 87.

53. Mundhenk, "Common Threads," 12.

54. Ibid.

complicated process involving manipulators, charms, rites and ceremonies, etc."[55]

The New Lion Handbook: The World's Religions claims that medicine men cult "died a natural death," and that chanting away "a spirit said to be causing sickness" for a fee "had been largely discontinued."[56] However the animistic worldview is not on the decline but on the rise in PNG. Following are some examples.

The animistic worldview, closely related to cult practices, is a growing problem among adolescents in the Secondary Private, and National High Schools.[57] This problem is present in boarding and day schools. A recent study has shown that "cult and its rituals and practices" have "become *de facto* standard practice in our schools."[58] One such practice is "name giving" where a year twelve student passes on the name to a new incoming year eleven student who then must behave according to the meaning of that name. Such names mostly have a negative impact on the young adolescent. A student shared with the church community at Pacific Adventist University his experience of being given a name *Spak* (Drunk), and he was expected to regularly drink alcoholic beverages to fulfill the meaning of his name.

Pacific Adventist University staff and church members have had to deal with demon possession on campus because of the adolescents who immersed themselves in practices such as killing a frog then drinking its blood and praying to Satan. In the beginning the "spirit" gave them powers—levitating a book from a second story house to the first, withdrawing money from a bank account without previously knowing the PIN (Personal Identification Number) number, and popularity with girls. Afterwards it required sacrifice of the life of the father and when obedience was denied, that adolescent displayed unusual, disturbed, and violent behavior.

---

55. Goodson, "Evangelizing," 59.
56. Partridge, *New Lion Handbook*, 109.
57. Department of Education, "Anti-Social," 3.
58. Drawii, "Cult," 86.

Part 1: Youth Ministry Challenge in PNG

I have heard students who have been involved in black magic giving testimonies. They differentiate black and white magic. White magic for them is harmless and positive, while black magic is negative and dangerous.

There was a staff member who had problems with their health—although all the tests showed that this person was healthy—and connected to it was the inability to open and read the Bible, pray, or say the name of Jesus, as that seemed to cause more sickness. It was believed that someone cast a spell on that person. It is a common practice when doctors cannot find anything wrong with a person, and the person is still suffering, to tell that person to find a sorcerer who will disclose who brought the trouble on them, and what to do in order to be released from the curse.

It is common to plant a certain tree near someone's house in order to chase away the evil spirit, or to carry a certain stone, leaf, feather, etc. for protection against the evil spirits or any bad sorcery that someone could place on another person, or to perform a ritual killing of a pig.[59] Neville Bartle, who lived as a missionary in PNG for thirty-two years, explains the Melanesian worldview by stating, "there is no clear dividing line between the spiritual world and the physical world, or between the visible world and the unseen world of the sprits: they are in constant interaction."[60] In this worldview, the living, the dead, and the unborn are present together, and the forests, together with the forest spirits, gardens with its spirits, and animals with their spirits, all form one world. Unlike the Western compartmentalized view where self is at the center and clearly separate compartments are those of art, education, transport, religion, economics, etc.

The death of a member of a clan will inevitably bring this worldview in focus. When there are unusual circumstances, or even without them, somebody will blame another person for the death that occurred. For example, Lucy's mum died recently after

---

59. See the explanation of the ritual killing of a pig near the Porgera mine to stop Coca-Cola bottles from being mysteriously emptied: Jacka, "Coca-Cola," 3–8.

60. Bartle, *Death*, 23.

an unsuccessful operation. Her brothers accused another family in the village of sorcery, and in revenge, attempted to kill the father and burned the house of that family. Even major Western companies, dealing with local landowners, experience problems with sorcery.[61]

In some areas it is believed that the spirit of the dead person will torment the living unless that person's death is avenged. This concept is known as payback. Sorcery plays an important part in payback techniques.[62] A sorcerer will be able to identify who is to blame for someone's death. When that happens, the identified culprit will have to be killed in order to appease the spirit of the dead person so that it will not torment the living. They will all be left in peace; however, that often starts a long payback legacy of killings between the clans.

Having to find the cause of all bad that happens, the cultures have found many explanations; for example, at Bosmun, dizziness is explained as "angry ancestors looking at you directly in the eyes." A stillborn child is explained in Karkar as "jealousy from a man who could not marry the mother."[63] To elucidate unusual events in life often related to death, which someone experienced during the day or night, it is claimed that *sanguma*, a spirit in the visible form or shape, is present.

Bartle shares several stories about *sanguma*. He tells of animals that turn into human beings and vice versa, dogs that come at night to eat a dead person's body, a pig that is shot who returns an arrow, a dog that is killed and a woman in another village dies instantly, a bat that enters a girl's chest when her mother dies, and many more.[64] They are stories that make people very fearful, and Christianity so far has not been able to effectively solve its mystery or overcome

61. Jacka, "Coca-Cola," 3–8.

62. Trompf, *Payback*, 60.

63. See ibid., 143–44, for a list of sicknesses with typically alleged causes, plus the culture in which that is found. See 148–49 for a list of deaths with alleged causes, when they are not caused in fighting. Most of these deaths are blamed on sorcery. An person dying of old age is the only one that is not seen as caused by external factors.

64. Bartle, *Death*, 219–64.

its power. In order to avoid trouble, preventative measures are sometimes taken. A banker, who is a prominent, active Christian, and a member of the SDA Church, told me that he is very careful when he goes to visit his family in the village where sorcery and *sanguma* is very strong. He makes sure that he gives money to all his relatives so that nobody will set any sorcery on him. "If a person is well off," he says, "and does not share his wealth with his relatives, the sorcerers will cause much trouble for that person."

This animistic worldview is prevalent in PNG and it is passed on through such experiences and stories that become more dramatic and invoke awe and fear. Often they are not shared with Westerners but they are shared among themselves. A young person grows up with these stories and experiences and has to adopt their lifestyle in accordance with them.

In an attempt to explain the influences that should inform and assist in developing the theology of youth ministry, this part has examined the context, influences, and ecology of where youth live in PNG. The diversity of the PNG context makes this task difficult. One can postulate that there must be norms that apply to all people, but that is not the case. This country is so rich in different cultures that "it is easy to distort the character of particular cultures cited, each one of which could absorb a lifetime's study."[65] So, when looking at context, influences, and ecology in PNG, one must keep in mind the vast differences that exist from place to place, from city to village, from highlands to islands.

A person growing up in a village will have a vastly different outlook on life from a person growing up in the city. They will wear different clothes, prepare food in a different way, eat different kinds of food, do different things, listen to different music, dance different styles of dances, attend different schools, if any, speak different languages, etc. The same could be said for those growing up in the islands and in the highlands, even in the way they are influenced by the media. Radio is the most available media

65. Trompf, *Payback*, 24.

Influences and Ecology

influence on all people in PNG, while television, internet, and print are much more restricted.

In every context of PNG, family, both immediate and extended, will play a significant role in the life of a young person. From their early days, young people will learn the rules of family functioning. In a village, these rules will be enforced with more authority than in the city, but in the city, one will rely more heavily on the *wantok* system. Underlying all these relationships and influences is the animistic worldview which to a larger or lesser degree binds a person. Although PNG is officially a Christian country, sorcery appears to be on the rise, with youth being especially vulnerable.

A youth pastor will need to carefully assess the context and influences that are applicable to each group, and based on that assessment, will need to adjust the work approach for each group. Unless a pastor does this preliminary assessment, they may not address the issues relevant to the group, and the group may eventually lose interest. This is not an easy task in such a diverse place where a pastor may care for ten or more churches. To be able to accomplish this task, it is of the utmost importance for the pastor to be firmly grounded in biblical principles. The next part of this book will explore youth ministry as practical theology in the SDA context, starting with the biblical call to adoption.

PART 2

Youth Ministry as Practical Theology in the SDA Context

CHAPTER 4

Biblical Call of Adoption and Practical Theology

THIS CHAPTER WILL EXAMINE the biblical view of family and youth ministry as a call to adoption, starting with the Old Testament's view of family, then including the rest of the Scriptures. It will move to point out how in practice several important issues have influenced youth ministry. The points of interest in this chapter will be eschatology, Americanism, and governance.

Biblical View of Family

According to the Bible, God created the first man and the woman and gave them the task of creating other human beings. He blessed the couple (Gen 1:28) and pronounced union between man and his wife very special (Gen 2:24). These are the first glimpses of family in the Old Testament, although the word "family" does not appear.

As with most topics of systematic theology, the Bible does not offer a study on family, instead, it shares stories of people's lives, and readers decide the moral of each story. These stories are imbedded in the history and culture of the people described, which sometimes makes the moral of the story difficult to determine. For example, because some stories talk about polygamous marriage, some conclude that God approves polygamy. However, by looking at the details of the stories, it is also easy to conclude that this is in fact not the case. Lamech, who started the trend of having more than one wife, did so in rebellion. Abraham, who succumbed to the traditional way of dealing with infertility, experienced family disagreements, dysfunction, pain, and divorce.

Adultery—having sex with someone who is not a legitimate spouse—is considered evil and punishable, but it is a temptation that concerns both men and women. Joseph is an example of one who refused to fall to that temptation (Gen 39:7–13). David is an example of one who fell. He did not realize the depth of his fall at first, but paid dearly for it (2 Sam 11–12).

Incest, another evil that distresses family, was strongly prohibited. Leviticus 18 and 20 give scenario after scenario of the kind of sexual relations not permitted. This indicates that God was concerned about the well-being of families and desired the best possible societal circumstances. These prohibitions are part of the laws given to the Israelites on their way to Canaan, where they would become one nation.

It is important to see what the term family meant in the Bible. The Hebrew term often translated as family, מִשְׁפָּחָה, is not what is generally understood to be a family in modern occidental society: father, mother, and children living in a house, separated from any other relatives. This Hebrew term is much broader, meaning clan, kindred, tribe, or nation.[1] The word that describes a smaller unit that would more closely relate to our meaning of family is בַּיִת, a house, a household, or בֵּית, a house of someone or something. However, even that term is often used for a larger unit that counts descendants or forefathers, slaves, and other workers.[2] Abram was able to call out the "318 trained men born in his household and went in pursuit" of four kings with their armies who took his nephew Lot captive (Gen 14:14).

---

1. Harris, *Theological Wordbook*, 947. Please note that not all the meanings for the original Hebrew and Greek words mentioned in this chapter are noted, but only those that are related to the topic of family.

2. Brown, *New*, 108–10. See also Harris, *Theological Wordbook*, 105.

Biblical Call of Adoption and Practical Theology

Children are considered a blessing from God. To be childless is seen as a curse. There are many words of wisdom on how to raise a child, especially in the book of Proverbs, and it is the duty of the family to raise a child. To witness grandchildren and great-grandchildren is the greatest fulfilment of life, "a crown to the aged" (Prov 17:6). Children need to be taught constantly. Moses repeated several times in the Pentateuch that the instructions given to the Israelites needed to be passed on to the next generation. "Impress them on your children. Talk about them when you sit at home and when you walk along the road, when you lie down and when you get up" (Deut 6:7). It is assumed that when each of these actions was happening, children would be with their parents, siblings, grandparents, or cousins—the Hebrew family. The result would be that they "may enjoy long life" (Deut 6:2).

The New Testament words οικος, and οικια, a house, can mean "all the persons forming one family," including the Christian church—"the family of God"—and also "stock, race, descendant of one."[3] Another word for family is πατρια, which means "lineage running back to some progenitor, ancestry," "a race or a tribe," and even wider "nation, people."[4] New Testament writers emphasize the "familial nature of the kingdom of God . . . God as Father of believers . . . believers as God's children . . . members of God's own family . . . through the work of the Holy Spirit, the spirit of adoption [where] Christ [is] their elder brother."[5] Therefore the New Testament not only follows on the understanding of a family as a large unit but expands that to the new Christian community. Those who for whatever reason lose their blood relatives can find new family in believers who share the same hope and who have the same mission in life. In other words, they can be adopted into the family of God, while they wait for real "adoption as sons, the redemption of our bodies" (Rom 8:23).

Adoption was not legislated in Old Testament times, although there are some examples of it, like Moses and Esther. Perhaps

3. Thayer, *New Thayer's*, 441.
4. Ibid., 495.
5. Williams, "Family," 245.

Part 2: Youth Ministry as Practical Theology in the SDA Context

children whose parents died were simply taken care of by their nearest relatives, as was the custom with wives whose husbands died (Deut 25:5). Although there is no Hebrew term for adoption, God often spoke of himself as a Father and of Israel and individuals in Hebrew history, like Solomon, as his sons.[6]

The New Testament audience, however, was much more acquainted with adoption, as "elaborate laws and ceremonies for adoption were part of both Greek and Roman society."[7] Paul used the term υιθεσια to describe how believers become the children of God, including all the privileges and obligations that this relationship brings. Freedom and inheritance in God's kingdom could easily be understood by his Roman audience where legal adoption brought equal freedom and rights as those of naturally born children.

The Bible has a special call to adoption. Each person who accepts Christ becomes his brother or sister, thus each believer becomes a brother or sister to one another and equally a child of God. Everyone is to put into practice Jesus' command to love one another as he loved first (John 13:34; 15:12). This call of adoption is particularly important in dealing with children and youth. After examining the biblical view of family and its significance for youth, the biblical view of youth ministry is looked at.

Biblical View of Youth Ministry

It is easily ascertained that there is no "youth ministry" mentioned in the Scriptures. However, that does not mean that the Bible says nothing about ministering to youth. Youth ministry is nested within the broad purpose of the church of making disciples (Matthew 28), building the kingdom of God (Luke 18:16–18), and the great outpouring of the Holy Spirit (Joel 2:28–29), where the hearts of parents will be turned toward their children and vice versa (Malachi 4:5–6).

---

6. Tasker, *Ancient*, 192.
7. Brown, "Adoption," 11.

Biblical Call of Adoption and Practical Theology

Young people are very important in the Bible. The Bible uses several terms to identify them.[8] They are often the ones who had a great commitment to God and great faith in God, and the ones whom God used for specific purposes. The Old Testament has several stories worth mentioning.

Joseph was young when he determined under very difficult circumstances to be faithful to God. He eventually became second in charge of the whole Egyptian kingdom and is a great example of forgiveness and reconciliation in family affairs (Genesis 37–50). David was a teenager when he showed great faith in God, facing a much larger and experienced enemy. He became the best known king in the history of the Jewish nation (1 Samuel 16–17; 2 Samuel).

Daniel decided in his youth to practice several spiritual disciplines throughout his life. He was firm on his choice of diet and prayer time under unfavorable circumstances. His firm stance paid off as he was well respected during two kingdoms, where he became known as a person of great wisdom and an interpreter of dreams. He also received visions about the future, which he wrote according to God's request for future generations of searchers for the true God (Daniel). Jeremiah and Samuel were both young when they accepted God's call to be his prophets and served God in that capacity throughout their lives (Jeremiah; 1 and 2 Samuel).

There was a young girl in Israel, whose name is not recorded, who was taken from her family in one of the raids of a neighboring army. It seems that what kept her strong was her faith. Not only that, but she also shared her faith in God, which produced a miraculous healing of her captor (2 Kings 5).

King Josiah, who was only eight years old when he became king, is an example of one faithful to God. In his time, the book of the law was found and he wholeheartedly listened to the advice given. He initiated much needed reformation that turned the whole nation to God (2 Kings 22–23).

---

8. According to Young, *Analytical Concordance*, 1084–85, different names are used for "young unmarried man" and woman, "growing young person," and "young person in the prime of life" in Hebrew and Greek.

Part 2: Youth Ministry as Practical Theology in the SDA Context

The New Testament is not short of examples. Timothy was a young man who worked alongside the great Apostle Paul. Four daughters of Philip are mentioned who had a prophetic gift. Mark, who wrote one of the gospels, was a young man when he started following Jesus and was later working with Paul and Barnabas in starting and building new churches. It is believed that perhaps half of Jesus' disciples were teenagers when he called them to follow him.

Jesus had strong messages for people dealing with young people. He told them, "Let the little children come to me, and do not hinder them" (Matt 19:14). He warned the people to be very careful not to cause them to sin, as "it would be better for him to have a large millstone hung around his neck and to be drowned in the depths of the sea" (Matt 18:6). From children, according to Jesus, can be learned how to be great in the kingdom of heaven—by having humbleness like that of a child (Matt 18:4). This kingdom belongs to those who are like children who want to come to Jesus (Matt 19:14). In Jesus' own words, children represent him: "Whoever welcomes a little child like this in my name welcomes me" (Matt 18:5).

Based on the Old and New Testament view of family and youth, the following principles emerge. First, every ministry in the church should have as the ultimate objective the making of disciples—followers of Christ. That would include development of character, understanding of the gospel and biblical teachings, and equipping for ministry and service to others (2 Tim 3:16–17). Second, youth ministry is nested in the overall ministry of the body of Christ, not something separate from the overall ministry and purpose of the local church, and it is in essence intergenerational. Third, youth ministry is missional and incarnational in nature, where, modeled by Christ's ministry to people, the church tries to understand the culture and adapt methods to that culture for the sake of reaching and impacting that culture. Fourth, youth ministry has a significant stewardship aspect, as children are gifts from God. Those working with youth are responsible to do that wisely as if ministering to Jesus. Fifth, adults should be careful not to become obstacles to youth coming to Christ. They should facilitate an environment where youth can be touched and blessed by Jesus, where they can gain the certainty of inheriting the kingdom. Sixth, youth ministry is to be proactive, initiating the search for youth just like Christ died for us "while we were still sinners" (Rom 5:8).

Thus far, the biblical basis for youth ministry was established by looking at what the Bible says about family and youth both in the Old and New Testaments. Youth are special to God and deserve the best efforts to bring them to God. Sometimes these efforts are greatly influenced by external agents or theological views. Three of these have been selected as the topics of the next part of this chapter.

This part of the chapter will identify the most significant and distinctive aspects of Adventism to see how these influenced the approach to practical ministry with youth. This will be limited to the SDA view of eschatology, the roots of Adventism as firmly based in the United States and as such transported to other parts of the world, and the centralized governance of the SDA Church.

Eschatology

The SDA Church has its origins in the Millerite movement of the 1840s when Jesus was expected to return on October 22, 1844. Especially significant Bible verses for the movement were from Revelation 14:6–12. They saw themselves as the fulfillment of that prophecy—the proclamation of the three angels' message—the last message to reach the earth before Jesus' second coming and the end of earth's history.[9]

Ever since the beginning of the movement, the main goal of the members of this church was to prepare people to meet Christ, whose coming was imminent. However, days turned into weeks, months, years, and even a century. Jesus has not yet returned, but the underlying message is still the same. It has touched every single youth in the church, who have asked questions like: Will I get married before Jesus comes? Will I finish school before Jesus comes? Will I pay off this loan before Jesus comes? Early Adventists

9. See Knight, *Anticipating the Advent*.

Part 2: Youth Ministry as Practical Theology in the SDA Context

thought that getting married was a sign of lack of faith in Jesus' return, that sending children to school was a waste of time and money, and that all their resources were to be used to warn the world of the end of time.

As time passed, however, marriage, education, and health became important again. The underlying reason for being involved in those was eschatological. Since Jesus was coming soon, children were educated to better understand the truths of the Bible. As husband and wife—a team—the couple would serve the community in being an example of God's love for this world, would share the news of Jesus' coming with others, and would raise children who would also join the kingdom of God. It became a duty of Adventists to take care of their health according to the message received from God through Ellen G. White, the church's prophetess, in order to have a better and longer life to proclaim Jesus' imminent return. These are the same reasons for initiating youth ministry.

The imminence of Jesus' return is a powerful motivator for mobilizing people to do outreach; however, it has its drawbacks. There seems to be a lack of time and resources to organize programs well. Preparations are hurried and superficial. For example, a school may be started in an area because there is evidence of a real need, but there is a lack of thorough planning, leaving the new school with not enough teachers, not enough books and other necessary resources to run successfully. The rush to get into these ventures seems to stem from the underlying urgency that Jesus is returning soon and our planet should be prepared for his coming.

Another drawback is the emotional high achieved with the rhetoric of the imminent coming of Christ. A person cannot function on an emotional high for a prolonged period of time. Those who plan their whole life around Jesus' return only, eventually find themselves on an emotional low and often leave the church with bitterness in their heart.

Americanism

It is a well-known fact that the SDA Church originated in the United States. Its base was initially in the eastern part of North America, in the New England states, from which it gradually spread west and southward. The advent message first crossed oceans as literature and only later missionaries were sent to Europe, Africa, Australia, Asia, and South America. Some were so excited about sharing this good news that they went without the church's blessing, while others were fully supported and officially sent.[10]

Perhaps similar to other Christian organizations of the time, it was not only the message that was shared, but the culture of the time was also passed on as gospel. Even today, American and English hymns are sung in Pacific churches; the Western dress code of suits, ties, and hats is worn to church; and church buildings resemble those of nineteenth-century America, not bearing similarity to the local culture. In some SDA Churches in PNG today church members still sing English hymns, although they do not understand the words. Preaching without a tie is seen as disrespectful to God, so a room next to the pulpit will have several ties, in case the preacher forgets to bring his own.

Literature that was printed in America was sent to other parts of the world. Soon translations started; nonetheless, translation into another language and adaptation to another culture is not the same thing. England and Australia, where English is the native language of most of the population, were sensitive to the American influence from the start, and were resistant to accept literature published in America. One of the publications with wide circulation was (and still is) the Sabbath School Lesson Pamphlet. For Australia and the South Pacific it is printed in Australia but is still prepared in America. Publishing houses across the globe publish it after it is translated into the local languages. The content still remains of American origin and flavor.

---

10. Michael B. Checzkowski and John Andrews, respectively, are two examples.

Part 2: Youth Ministry as Practical Theology in the SDA Context

When youth ministry started in PNG, especially through Pathfinders, the enthusiasm in the meetings came from singing American songs, especially the Scripture in Song series. The textbooks were from America. The awards were from America, and corresponded to the types of activities that American children would be involved in.

It is not surprising that this was the trend, since the Church started in the United States, but the second reason was financial. As the church grew, growth was largest in the United States where the finances were also the greatest. Therefore, it was natural that those with resources would share them with others outside. They shared what they learned and discovered in the context of their culture, passing it on as the truth, not realizing the long-term effect of that approach. Today this trend continues, although there is much local adaptation and local talent influencing the church culture. American influence is present in some ways even more today, not only in the church but in society in general through Internet, television, radio, and other readily available media, and youth especially are greatly influenced by it.

Governance

The SDA Church has gone through several stages of organization. It started with rejecting any kind of formal organization because it was believed that any form of church organization was Babylon of Revelation 18 and 14:8. However, the "pragmatic need for some form of organization certainly was the impetus needed to force" the pioneers to organize in some form: they had a printing press and a publishing house that needed to be registered in someone's name.[11] James White, who was the force behind the publishing venture, did not want to have those assets in his private name, thus they had to choose the name of the organization and form a company. That was the first step towards organization.

---

11. Oliver, *SDA*, 47.

Biblical Call of Adoption and Practical Theology

By 1863, the early Adventists had several churches that organized themselves into groups of churches, called conferences, with leaders emerging. After several years of debating the pros and cons of organization, the General Conference was formed as the governing body of the Church, together with the first president, John Byington. Apart from a two-year experiment in 1900, the SDA Church has had a General Conference president ever since.[12]

The initial governing structure of the church-conference-general conference was enlarged in the early 1900s by adding another level, the union conference. Subsequently, the General Conference was divided into world districts called divisions and today there are thirteen divisions. Each Division president is a de facto General Conference vice president. In theory, divisions are not considered another layer of church governance, although in practice it is hard to differentiate the two.

The way this organization of churches operates is that each church has leaders for certain ministry areas, such as personal ministry, youth ministry, or children's ministry. A group of churches that belongs to a conference would have its representatives for decision making from these groups. Each conference would have leaders in these same areas to support local churches in these ministries. The same scenario would be replicated in the union conference, division office, and General Conference. Depending on the size of the church/conference/union, some would take care of one or several ministries. When this system was established, it was very efficient. However, today it seems overly administrative and hard to change.

The structure and governance of the church is democratic.[13] The majority of members of the executive boards are chosen

---

12. A list of all presidents can be found in Herbert Douglass, *Messenger of the Lord* (Nampa, ID: Pacific Press Publishing Association, 1998), to which should be added the current president, Ted Wilson, who was elected in 2010. This list is also found at *Wikipedia*, s.v. "List of Presidents of the General Conference of Seventh-day Adventists," accessed September 25, 2011, online: http://en.wikipedia.org/wiki/List_of_Presidents_of_ the_General_Conference_of_Seventh-day_Adventists.

13. "World Church Structure and Governance," Adventist.org, accessed

through an election process. Sessions are held every three years for the conferences while General Conference in its full form meets quinquennially. The last General Conference Session was in July 2010, in Atlanta, Georgia, USA, where over two thousand delegates from all over the world met to discuss issues and vote on numerous agenda items. The last Sabbath program was attended by around seventy thousand church members.

This level of organization has produced great work in the past. The SDA Church can boast the largest Protestant education system and extensive medical work with many hospitals and clinics around the globe. It has publishing houses, food factories, development and relief agencies, satellite television, media centers, and many other services.[14] There is much for church members to be proud of and satisfied with if they take into account how much the church has developed and in how many ways it has impacted the world for the better.

At the same time, it appears as huge machinery which has been developed and is now functioning seemingly without necessarily fulfilling the original mission it had. When a new idea is developed it takes a long time to pass it into action, as it needs to go through several layers of boards to be approved. The experiences the church has gone through have urged it to develop policies to protect its workers and itself, which today may sometimes be restrictive and self-protective.[15] There are procedures in place to safeguard the unchangeability of the whole system. To change a policy can take years. For those working with youth, who are part of the quickly changing world, this may be a very restrictive atmosphere to work in.

The biblical call of adoption is clear. Children and youth are important to God, both seen in the Old and New Testaments of

September 25, 2011, online: http://www.adventist.org//world-church/facts-and-figures/structure/index.html.

14. For a summary of facts and figures, see the official SDA website: http://www.adventiststatistics.org.

15. The church has a Ministers Manual, Workers Policy, Occupational Health and Safety Policy, Church Manual, Job Descriptions, Wages Schedule, and a host of other policies and procedures.

the Bible. They are God's gift to people. This is a solid basis for the church as a community to be wholeheartedly involved and interested in their well-being. Added to that is the sacrifice of Jesus for each one of them, his example of dealing with them, and his call to discipleship.

Practical theology as discussed in this chapter is seen through three main aspects: eschatology, Americanism, and governance. The underlying element in Adventist theology is its view of eschatology, the imminence of Jesus' second coming, and the urgency that belief puts on everything. The theology and practice in the church was exported from America, therefore an American flavor is present in all its activities. By now, the church has developed a strong system of governance, which is beneficial in certain areas and deterring in others. To still further understand youth ministry as practical theology in the SDA context, the history of youth ministry in the church needs to be addressed. The following chapter will look at that history in the SDA Church at large, and also in PNG in particular.

CHAPTER 5

Youth Ministry History in the SDA Church

THE SDA CHURCH STARTED with young people. Ellen White (then Harmon), one of the founders, was only seventeen when she received her first vision, in 1844, and started sharing it with others.[1] Many young people actively served in the progress of the fledgling group. James White, John Nevins Andrews, John Loughborough, and others were in their early twenties. How the relationship between church and youth evolved through the years will be explored in this chapter, first looking at the history of youth ministry in the SDA Church, with its beginnings in the United States and then expansion in PNG.

Youth Ministry History in the SDA Church at Large

The first attempt to target youth as a specific group with materials specially prepared for them was very early in the SDA Church history.[2] Most members of the group were disturbed with the consequences of their failed expectation of Jesus' return. They were trying

---

1. There are several books dealing with the history of the SDA Church that contain the data presented in this statement. See, e.g., Schwarz and Greenleaf, *Light Bearers*.

2. This started when the SDA Church did not exist as an organized entity and was not known by that name. The SDA Church was officially registered 10 years later, in 1863, with this name chosen on October 1, 1861.

72

to clarify what they believed and in that search neglected the youth. James White was concerned for the youth. The first issue of *The Youth's Instructor* came off the press in 1852. *The Youth's Instructor* was printed once a month, and its eight pages were "designed to provide weekly Sabbath School lessons on doctrinal topics and other reading material" that would be interesting and instructive to children.[3] In 1869, Goodloe Harper Bell produced separate lessons for children and youth which influenced its audience for almost thirty years. It was, however, another half a century until more serious and strategic work for youth was to start.

Two teenagers are generally considered originators of the first Adventist Young People's Society. Luther Warren, who was fourteen at the time, and Harry Fenner, seventeen, formed the first youth group in 1879, in their home in Hazelton, Michigan, "to help their young friends experience spiritual birth or revival."[4] Warren later (1894) organized Sunshine Bands to direct young people in missionary work.[5] As these bands grew, it was obvious that the church needed to organize an official young people's department. At first this was done in conjunction with the already established Sabbath School Department. It was not long till this partnership was no longer sufficient, and in 1907, the Young People's Department of the General Conference was created with Milton E. Kern as its director, Matilda Erickson as secretary, and a seven-member advisory committee.[6]

The organization was concerned with preparing materials helpful to young people and those working with them. The following years saw the publishing of the Reading Course, Standard of Attainment, and Morning Watch, which was very popular.[7]

3. Schwarz and Greenleaf, *Light Bearers*, 75.
4. Holbrook, *AY Story*, 2.
5. Erickson, *Missionary*, 13–14.
6. Schwarz and Greenleaf, *Light Bearers*, 320.
7. This Reading Course was a selection of books for spiritual and educational reading. Standard of Attainment was a series of studies, and Morning Watch was a calendar with one verse from the Bible to be read each morning. The circulation of the Morning Watch Calendar soared from 6,000 to 33,000 copies in four years.

Part 2: Youth Ministry as Practical Theology in the SDA Context

Another interesting pamphlet was developed, in the form of small leaflets covering instructive and inspirational topics relevant to youth, called Missionary Volunteer Leaflet Series.

Kern organized a convention in the same year he was elected as director, which selected the name for the new society within the church: Seventh-day Adventist Young People's Society of Missionary Volunteers later shortened to MVs. The convention selected "three major aims: to develop devotional life, missionary endeavour, and educational activities."[8] It was during this convention that an aim, a motto, and a pledge for the society were adopted. *The Youth's Instructor* was recognized as its official magazine. The call was raised for an annual Week of Prayer, specifically for youth, and for conferences to organize Missionary Volunteer Departments with full-time leaders.[9]

It was soon obvious that youth work required skilled workers, so in 1913 the General Conference session resolved to organize a special form of training for them. They also formed Junior Missionary Volunteer societies—JMVs. Further, this year was significant because goals were set for what the youth needed to achieve, and most goals were not only attained before the deadline, but surpassed.

The work with youth mushroomed in the next ten years: the number of societies tripled, membership in those tripled, hours of community service grew over twenty-seven times, and offerings for outreach ministry grew over twenty-nine times, with the average contribution per person growing over ten times.[10] This work spread outside of the United States to Europe, the South Pacific, India, Southeast Asia, the Philippines, China, Japan, Korea, South America, Africa, and the Caribbean. New leadership and new ideas were fuelling the growth. Activities such as camping, hikes, outdoor games and crafts were adopted as excellent tools to reach youths. A. W. Spaulding started organizing "Mission Scouts" in 1919, which became the basis for Pathfinders. Harriet Holt ex-

8. Schwarz and Greenleaf, *Light Bearers*, 320.
9. Ibid.
10. Holbrook, *AY Story*, 24. Information in the following paragraphs is taken from the same book.

perimented with a small club of girls, which helped her to develop the requirements for the curriculum for the new program: Friend and Companion in the JMVs and Comrade and Master Comrade in the MVs (later called Guide and Master Guide). Special scarves and small pins (later patches) were given to those who completed the requirements.

From these beginnings, the work for youth grew and changed with time. In the 1940s the Medical Cadet Corps (MCC) was developed and incorporated into the MV Department. It was designed to teach young men and women to be good medical soldiers for their country while remaining in God's army. Henry Bergh wrote the "Pathfinder Song," which is still sung today. By 1950, the Pathfinder Program was accepted worldwide. Soon after, the first Pathfinder Camporees were organized, and they continue still.[11] The MV Honor program grew from sixteen to 150 honors by 1957. Another more challenging honor was added in 1958, called the Silver Award, which combined physical, mental, and cultural challenges for high school–age youth. The Gold Award, even more difficult, followed for college-age youth to test the physical capabilities of those who wanted to excel as athletic, physically fit Christians. In the early 1960s, colleges started sending students on mission trips ranging from a few weeks to a whole year of community service somewhere in the mission field—Africa, Asia, Latin America, and the islands of the South Pacific. In the late 1960s, the church started hosting camps for blind youth, a novelty at the time, but of great impact on thousands of young blind persons and those working with them.

Not all was well in the 1960s. What used to be a practical, mission-oriented program changed into an entertainment-style program, filling in Sabbath hours, so that youth would not break the behavior rules of Sabbath. However, as youth found other more interesting ways of entertaining themselves, church attendance

---

11. The latest camporee, as reported by Garcia-Marenko in "Adventist Camporee," 6–7, had an attendance of twenty thousand Pathfinders from thirty-four countries in the Inter-American Division (IAD) territory who participated in a six-day camporee in Mexico City from April 19–23, 2011.

dropped, and their interest in youth programs diminished. The need for change became obvious.

In 1979, the name of the youth organization changed from MV—Missionary Volunteer to AY—Adventist Youth, and from JMV—Junior Missionary Volunteer to AJY—Adventist Junior Youth. It was around this time that a new curriculum was launched for "pre-JMV." The Adventurer Club, a parent-child-oriented program, fully independent of the Pathfinder Club, was aimed at children in the first four grades of elementary school. The senior youth received another curriculum, separate from the Master Guide—Youth Leadership Award. To that was added the Pathfinder Leadership Award and the Advanced Pathfinder Leadership (or Instructor) Award as two levels of continuing education for Master Guides. Big events like Youth Congresses, Pathfinder Camporees, and Festivals of Faith were organized throughout different divisions, which brought together youth from different countries, excellent speakers, musicians, and drama performers to make those events memorable and inspirational.

In more recent times, big events are still very important and happen on a more regular basis. Division-wide camporees or youth congresses happen every three to five years. These events are more community oriented as youth engage in working together to impact the community. This includes community outreach through singing, preaching, distribution of literature, programs for children, and development projects such as building, painting, cleaning, and tree planting, all running parallel with the main event. Smaller events are happening throughout the churches. Some are requirements for Pathfinder honors; some like StormCo—Service To Others Really Matters Company—are once-a-year events to strengthen the youth.[12]

Technology has influenced work with youth. In 2002, the GC Youth Department launched a website full of resources for youth work.[13] Two years later, the then president of GC, Jan

---

12. For more details about StormCo, see their website: http://stormco.adventistconnect.org.

13. See the Youth Ministries Department of the General Conference of

Paulsen, started a dialogue with youth called "Let's Talk," which was broadcast through Hope Channel, openly discussing issues of interest to the youth.

Youth in the church today can go through extended Leadership Training program. They may start while teenagers, followed by the Master Guide program and the Pathfinder Leadership Award. These programs equip them for church and community leadership.

To assess the state of affairs in the youth department, research was conducted in this area. Some of the specialists in youth work were Roger Dudley and Bailey Gillespie, followed by Barry Gane, each of whom has researched youth work and written books and articles on the matter. Valuegenesis was one such research project, first conducted in 1989 in SDA schools in North America in the areas of family, school, and church. "The impact of the study set in motion a whole series of events—planned changed conferences, vision-to-action focus groups, new concerns, attitudes, training programs, priorities of the home, school, and church, and publications—that resulted in more effective ways to help youth to a life of commitment and loyalty to the Adventist church."[14] Since the first research, another round was conducted in 2000, and a third in 2010. Same research was later also carried out in Europe and Australia.

The church is interested in youth and is trying to find ways of working with and for youth. In different parts of the world, different strategies are used and different work is conducted. The following section is an exposition of how the youth work progressed in the SDA Church in PNG.

SDA online: http://gc.bigfoottech.com.

14. See "Valuegensis," on the John Hancock Center for Youth and Family Ministry at La Sierra University's website, accessed November 23, 2011, online: http://www.lasierra.edu/centers/hcym.

Part 2: Youth Ministry as Practical Theology in the SDA Context

Youth Ministry History in the SDA Church in PNG

It would be good to say that youth ministry in PNG started at the same time as the missionaries started sharing their SDA beliefs; however, there is no indication that this was so, at least not intentionally. The year 1908 is considered the beginning of the SDA Church in PNG, although it was many years until the first convert was baptized.[15]

It is generally accepted today that youth ministry in PNG started in 1957 with the arrival of Kevin Silva from Australia, who introduced JMV and MV clubs to Jones Missionary College, now called Kambubu Secondary School.[16] However, work started earlier, as can be seen in this quote from the 1956 Australasian Record describing the first Sepik camp meeting:

> The young people and JMV's also found their full satisfaction in their MV activities, and were ably led by Mrs. Lemke and Mrs. Raethel. The ability of the youth to master this work was demonstrated in our special MV programme on Sabbath afternoon, when, to the great pleasure of the hundreds of fathers and mothers present, they were able to hear their young people recite their memory work of the progressive classes. We were also privileged to have Pastor Ken Gray with us from our union college. His enthusiasm in MV activities is catching, and it would appear that these people have caught it. . . .
>
> [During the afternoon mission meeting offering appeal] the young people marched around in *the usual way*, bringing their offerings to the front; and the adults were so taken with the idea that they soon joined the marching throng.[17]

15. In 2008, there were big celebrations for the centenary of the SDA Church's work in PNG. I participated in some of those events.

16. Information regarding the history of PNG youth work is mainly derived from two sources: interviews with Matupit Darius, Kadasa Damaro, and Daniel Lavaiamat, conducted on October 7 and 12 and December 14, 2010, at Pacific Adventist University, Port Moresby, PNG; and Thelma Silva, wife of the late Kevin Silva, who wrote a chapter in a teaching resource for Master Guide Program for the South Pacific Division in April 2010.

17. Lemke, "First," 9 (italics not in the original).

Already, in 1957, there were six hundred reported MV clubs with several members completing the requirements for the courses.[18] One of the men who received the first badges in the 1950s is Ponu, who still lives on Manus Island.

The wives of missionaries had a big influence on the children and young adults as they worked with them during Sabbath and daily worships. Hugh A. Dickins described daily worship in 1956: "Every day in the coolness of the morning, in every Adventist village from palm fringed shore to those perched precariously on mountain heights, you will hear the church bell ringing the people to worship, to the study of the morning watch, and the Sabbath school lesson. It is their daily and firmly established habit."[19] The same routine was followed in the schools established, as it is through formal education that the church was trying to influence the youth during the early stages of its work among the PNG people.

Pathfindering was a significant way through which churches intentionally worked with youth. Daniel Lavaiamat expressed it concisely: "Youth work meant Pathfindering."[20] Kevin Silva started the first Pathfinder Club in Australia in 1953, so when he was appointed to work in PNG in 1957, he was keen to start Pathfinder clubs there, too. His work for the youth of PNG lasted till 1990, when he retired. It was of such importance that he was awarded the PNG Independence Medal for his services to the youth of PNG in 1985.[21] He wrote textbooks, manuals, flow charts, yearly planners, and handbooks, incorporating PNG honors like basket weaving, canoeing the traditional PNG way, and PNG crafts, as well as adapting available materials from America or Australia to the PNG setting.

Silva, however, was not the first one to officially start working with youth. Around 1945, Marie Pascoe already conducted JMV classes in Bougainville, and Tutty had done the same in Manus,

18. Campbell, "Savages," 1.

19. Dickins, "Why," 3.

20. Daniel Lavaiamat, interview by author, December 14, 2010, Pacific Adventist University, Port Moresby, PNG.

21. Silva, "History," 13–17.

Part 2: Youth Ministry as Practical Theology in the SDA Context

where young people's meetings were held each Sabbath afternoon. Later, Ken Gray, together with Hugh Dickens, prepared local honors and included many local people to help in the work with youth.

Those appointed to work with youth generally had other portfolios, especially education, until Lewis Lansdown was specifically and solely given responsibilities for youth work in PNG in 1975. He established Pathfinder fairs, camps, and camporees, which greatly increased the interest of youth. He invited well-known youth leaders from America to attend such events, which further established youth work.

As education work progressed with the establishment of new schools so, too, did youth work grow. Completing the Master Guide program was compulsory at Kambubu and later Sonoma schools. When these students completed their studies, they were equipped to start JMVs and Pathfinders in places where they were appointed to work.

By the 1980s youth work was the leading avenue for evangelism, and church membership exploded, especially in the Highlands. "Voice of Youth" was a name given to programs that youth organized for evangelistic programs. Youth organized new churches, and in many of these there was no grey head to be seen. Camps for youth were organized, Friday Night Fellowships (FNF) were regular and well-attended meetings for youth and by youth. New songs from Scripture in Song were well received. Youth formed choirs and visited other churches. Street preaching became very popular, too. Youth quizzes, testimonies, sermons, group singing, community work, and evangelism were new mediums of youth involvement.

In 1985, the PNG Youth Congress was held with the King's Heralds as special guests from overseas. Due to this event, many youth who had previously left the church joined the SDA youth force again. Another important change occurred in the structure of the church when the Church Ministries Department was organized with Youth Ministry under its umbrella. The first local youth leader was Tomita Sumatau.

PNGATSA (Papua New Guinea Adventist Tertiary Students Association) was organized in 1983. The purpose was to spiritually and physically support each other.²² It was to be an organization for and by students. PNGATSA has other chapters in the country who organize various activities and support for tertiary students in PNG.²³

Today, youth and child work are divided into the following sections: six- to nine- year-olds have Adventurers; ten- to fifteen-year-olds have Pathfinders; sixteen- to twenty-one-year olds can join Ambassadors, and ages twenty-two to thirty-one are considered youth or young adults, and work with them has to do with equipping them for leadership. The SDA Church has well-established programs for young people, far better organized than other churches in PNG.²⁴ Each administrative section of church work in PNG appoints a youth leader for that area.

Changes in the society are providing many new challenges and possibilities for youth work in PNG. Based on what is happening now, one can try to project what will be happening in the future. The following chapter will discuss future trends, as may be currently anticipated.

22. Warren Marape, "PNGATSA," 1.

23. An example is SASA, Simbu Adventist Student Association, who are very serious about their work. See "Constitution of the 'Simbu Adventist Student Association," accessed November 20, 2011, online: http://www.sasaleva.com/Final%20Draft-%20Revised%20SASA%20Constitution%5B1%5D.pdf.

24. Daniel Lavaiamat strongly pointed out this issue. He was asked by other churches to help them establish their youth programs, as they do not have them but see the need. The SDA Church is also considered to have the best education system, and many parents from a non-SDA background are sending their children to SDA schools. Demand is far greater than supply.

CHAPTER 6

Anticipated Trends

IT IS NECESSARY TO look at history to understand the present. What is happening today is not happening in a vacuum, it has been influenced by the past. Also, by looking at the present and looking wide, one can anticipate the future. This chapter will analyze the SDA Church at large and then specifically the scene in PNG.

SDA Church At Large

In his article "Courage to Lead," Branimir Schubert identified several societal changes that impact the church and proposed actions for leaders.[1] Those societal influences are instability, fast pace of change, energy shortage, growing social and economic gap, clash of values between different generations, new decision-making environment, innovation, and trust/authenticity/role modeling. These currents in society affect the church. The most important issues affecting the church, Schubert identified as identity, disproportionate growth, finances, governance, youth, women, de-institutionalization, and interconnectivity. These issues, and how they relate to work with youth, are explored further.

---

1. Schubert, "Courage," 8–12.

Identity—"Who am I?" is not only an issue which adolescents are dealing with, the SDA Church is dealing with the same issue.² The main purpose for the SDA Church was to warn people of Jesus' second coming. That is now over 160 years ago, and many generations who believed Jesus would come in their time have long been buried. The urgency of that message has somewhat waned. Another important message was health reformation. Today governments are preaching what the SDA Church was preaching a hundred years ago. Adventists have dropped their standards, and their health statistics now match that of the general population in overweight, stress levels, their loosened view on alcohol drinking, and meat consumption. Parents' attitudes will probably be reflected in the attitudes and behaviors of youth.

Disproportionate growth—the church is growing in the developing world but declining in the developed world. In South America, Africa, East Asia, and the Pacific, the number of baptisms is growing daily, while in Europe, North America, and Australia there is almost a negative growth when taken into account those who leave the church or die. This disproportionate growth affects church finances, governance and how women are viewed. This also means that what is important to youth in one area is not necessarily so in another. When events are organized where youth from different cultures come together, the younger ones have hard times coping with such vast differences.³

Finances—the church is growing in the areas where finances are in meager supply. The church is not growing fast in the areas of the world where finances, although shaken by the global economic crisis, are still in good shape. There are not enough funds to accommodate the needs of the growing areas. That brings about tension.

---

2. A Google search on November 21, 2011, for "Adventist identity crisis" returned 52,200 hits, with links to conferences, sermons, articles, blogs, and books. This number will probably increase in the future.

3. Some examples of this: Daniel Lavaiamat commented on dress code in Australia, which greatly disturbed PNG youth who came for camporee; and when the Underground series was filmed and broadcasted throughout the Pacific, many Pacific people negatively commented that it was geared towards an Australian audience but broadcasted in the Pacific, too.

Part 2: Youth Ministry as Practical Theology in the SDA Context

This may be particularly disturbing younger generations who like to see immediate changes brought about with their finances. They may give to the church but may not understand the bigger picture. When financial statements are seen, those from developing countries may not understand how the money is distributed and how expensive some things are in Western countries. They may form a false view of how "rich" the church is and be disappointed when their projects are not financed.[4]

Governance—it is based on history and policies. This will need to change to accommodate new ideas, renewed mission, and innovative projects. Policies will have to be rewritten or altogether discarded. Youth need to be more involved in official meetings of the church and church leaders need to be more involved with the youth if mutually agreeable outcomes are expected in this area in the future.

Youth—in some parts of the world congregations are old and getting older, while in other parts they are young. This does not necessarily mean young in age. In some parts, churches are well established with traditions that cannot be broken, while there are places where new churches are springing up. If these are in the same general area, it is very hard to meet together, as the differences between the two congregations seem insurmountable. Those who are old in traditions or age are dying out—from Sabbath to Sabbath, pews are emptier.[5] On the other hand, if members of young congregations do not feel welcome to attend older established ones,

---

4. During the year-end meetings in the South Pacific Division November 8–10, 2011, the president took time to carefully explain the financial statements to the delegates from the Pacific. Those who have a financial background were happy with how the church is managing the funds. Hopefully the others could also communicate a positive message to their constituency after hearing the explanation from the president.

5. On Sabbath, November 19, 2011, I was at Vallejo Drive SDA Church in Glendale. On seeing several rows of front pews empty, I asked a church member who attended that church for the past thirty years whether they will be filled. She replied that they would not. She commented that previously there was no seating space, as the church was full, but currently it was getting emptier. This is just one random supportive example.

Anticipated Trends

it creates division in the church, which challenges unity that the church is very strongly trying to accomplish.

Women—still form the majority of church members in male-dominated leadership. There is a big discrepancy between the status of women in the developed world and the still-developing world. Since the church is democratic and representative in its constitution, delegates from the developing world have the majority of votes. For several decades now, women's leadership potential was denied due mainly to this difference in opinions. This is detrimental in some parts of the world, as it affects not only women but also the youth. It does not seem that the situation will change in the near future, as yet another issue of women in leadership was voted down at the latest meetings of the General Conference.[6] Youth are voicing their concerns about this issue, which is a good sign; however, there are those who do not speak up but simply leave the church.

De-institutionalization—new generations look for leaders that have earned their respect. Time has passed when leaders held people's respect because of their positions. The Church is built on a hierarchical system, with presidents and directors. They need to gain the respect of young people if they want the authority.

Interconnectivity—the spread of news through social media and not necessarily through official channels is a great force for either good or evil, both of which have been seen in recent times.[7] Young people are born in this world of interconnectivity. Those who lead them need to understand this realm and help them to use it productively for the benefit of others.

Another issue that is important to mention, which Schubert did not include, is postmodernity. All youth are born in this paradigm, which is very different from modernity. While older people have seen and experienced the change, youth are born in this new world, and their worldview is totally different to the leaders of the

---

6. Kellner, "Variance," n.p.

7. One of the main influences in the Arab Spring upheavals and British street protests of 2011 has been that of the social media. Arguably the first one was a good influence and the second a negative one.

Part 2: Youth Ministry as Practical Theology in the SDA Context

church today. For a church that boasts having the truth, it is difficult to convince a postmodern person who does not believe in absolute truth. This is only one of the issues faced by youth and their leaders. "Further renewal is vital to make the Adventist community in many places less judgmental and more embracing and inclusive, defining and defending important principles rather than focusing on rules and regulations that everyone must strictly adhere to; urging its members to apply those principles in a radical way to the challenges of our 'present' world."[8]

SDA Church in PNG

PNG has changed dramatically during the last five years; both young people and their parents are struggling to cope. Technology has opened wide the doors to Western influences, especially to the youth, while parents and elders are still clinging to past traditions and culture. This struggle is evident in different ways. A recent example of violence at PAU is one such indication. A security guard who was supposed to provide protection to a female student on a path unseen by other security personnel attempted to rape her, then attacked her with an axe when she resisted. Later on, students attacked this security guard in retaliation.[9] This is not an isolated, nor the worst case, in the world of violence in Port Moresby and PNG. Although this story is disturbing and very negative, positive comments were also given by a student: "PAU stand still n let God move!!!!!! may d Lord see this through n lead n b glorified!" and five minutes later "Stand still n let God move!!!!!!!!!!!"[10] A teen also remarked: "Things that happen at PAU should remain in PAU! No need to update everyone in the city! Thass how stories twist & turn out to be something totally

---

8. Reinder Bruinsma discusses this topic from an Adventist perspective in "Present Truth Revisited." At the time of writing, this was still an unpublished manuscript. The quote is from p. 167 of this document.

9. This story was printed in the newspapers. See Muri, "Guard," n.p.

10. Posted to Facebook by Suinite Pole on November 20, 2011, at 6:29 and 6:34 p.m. via mobile phone.

different! If only people could think before they post up things on their status! GROW UP CHILDISH ADULT!"[11]

Other things are more attractive to young people than well-established Pathfinders and Master Guide programs. They prefer to send text messages through mobile phones and comment on social networks to each other, discuss the latest movies or play with new gadgets. Although they still like to sing, it is now in a new style. More disturbing than a new style is a spirit of competition among the singing groups in the city rather than a spirit of praising God.[12]

There is a big and ever-growing gap between youth who grow up in the village and those from the city. Those in a village are still under the influence of the whole village, and the whole village is interested in the well-being of each child. There is a sense of community, of one culture, one direction. In the city are many cultures and less community involvement. The attitude of church members toward someone's child is *Em i no pikinini blo mi*—meaning, "this is not my child, not my problem, does not need my involvement"—which is a problematic attitude in a culture where community is so important. Those in the village still hear the morning and evening bells calling them to worship, prayer, and Bible reading. In the city there are no such bells, life is busy, and children are often left alone to fend for themselves while parents are occupied in formal or informal employment.

Staff in the education system are now remunerated by the government, even teachers in SDA schools, both in the villages and cities. This is of great concern, for it seems to cause them not to be fully committed to Adventist education principles. There is more emphasis on theory than practical daily living.

Those in churches who are elected to work with youth, especially teenagers, consider them too difficult to work with and often quit even though it only requires one hour a week during Sabbath

---

11. Posted to Facebook by Princes Lalita (Facebook username, not real name) on November 21, 2011, via mobile phone.

12. Lavaiamat and Damaro, interviews, 2010.

Part 2: Youth Ministry as Practical Theology in the SDA Context

School.[13] The more traditional churches follow old routines in an authoritative way. Either way is not working, as youth attend such meetings less and less and tend to rather stay home or meet their friends elsewhere. Once they are old enough to leave their parents' home, they stop attending church, although some of them come back to church once they have a family of their own.

For those families who have joined the church recently and who have not experienced the church education system, who do not have firmly established habits of family worship, do not transmit these values to their children. They rely on the church to provide spiritual food. It is not enough to discuss spiritual matters only on Sabbath mornings.

There is a growing trend of occultism, especially in high school settings and universities. Although in schools they teach much scientific knowledge, when it comes to spirituality, they are turning back to the roots of PNG spirituality. Sorcery and black and white magic have lingered underneath the facade of Christianity, and are now resurfacing.

Some youth are not coping with the changes in society. The difference between what their parents are teaching and requiring of them, and the information they receive through the media is so vast that they do not see a way forward and some decide to just end their lives. Suicides are increasing, presently, even in the church. Suicides are not reported in the newspapers, while murders, rapes, and burglaries are. Kadasa Damaro described several recent suicides in the area he comes from.[14] The most recent (October 2010) was in his own family—his cousin hanged himself. As a young man, he was following what he saw in the

---

13. This was my experience at PAU. For the four years that I was in charge of the teen Sabbath School, nobody wanted to take on that leadership. I became involved and then took on the leadership because I was concerned about my son and other children's spiritual lives. Whenever I approached people to join the team, the answer was always negative. I had two to three reliable people working with me during that period and there ware about fifty teens to work with. Many Sabbaths I was alone with them.

14. Kadasa Damaro, interview by author, October 12, 2010, Pacific Adventist University, Port Moresby, PNG.

Western movies—young people holding hands, walking together, hugging, while his mother told him that he is not meant to do that. "He was torn between two belief systems." Damaro pointed out that there are two ways of committing suicide, depending on the area one is from: hanging in the villages, and an overdose of medicine in the cities.[15]

PNG society is struggling to come to terms with the outbreak of AIDS and prospects for the future are grim. Although more people are infected in the cities, villages are not spared from the outbreak, as people move a lot between village and city. Because of the lack of education there is more stigma attached to AIDS sufferers in the villages, especially women. Youth are easy prey to promiscuous adults who promise money or gadgets in return for sexual favors. Youth workers in the church need to address this issue, pointing to the benefits of a pure life, including the enjoyment of sex within the boundaries of marriage. The church may find itself losing a portion of youth to AIDS and gaining a whole generation of orphans.

What used to be unheard of issues are becoming common: marriage break-ups, elopements, premarital sex, and unwanted pregnancies. What makes matters worse is that relationship issues, especially sexual intimacy, are still taboo topics, something not talked about in families. Youth are not informed by elders, parents, or church officers, but are left to the influence of Hollywood movies where sex is promoted as a leisure activity, where partners are exchanged based on shallow attractions. There is no process where youth can discuss those issues with trusted adults who can give them a wider perspective.

The SDA Church boasts having the truth and being a chosen people with a mission for the last days before Jesus returns. The great emphasis on doctrines is, however, not touching the hearts and minds of the youth. The way that truth is presented is not attractive or meaningful to young people.

---

15. Chloroquine and amoxicillin are two examples, but he said that any medicine that you take ten to fifteen tablets of can kill you, and youth know that.

Part 2: Youth Ministry as Practical Theology in the SDA Context

The youth of PNG are embracing technological advances wholeheartedly. Mobile phones have transformed the country in the last five years. Although it is easy to point out the negative influence this can have, especially through transmission of pornographic material, its potential to move youth is great and needs to be used. Current church leadership is not as tech savvy as the youth they are supposed to lead. Youth need to have trained, committed leaders who will communicate with them on their level through means they use to communicate among themselves. They need local heroes and role models to lead them. They need a church that embraces them, acknowledges and cherishes their talents; where they are part of the community.

In many ways the future is determined by plans made now or in the past. The PNG government has set up a National Strategic Plan 2010–2050. Their vision is that "Papua New Guinea is a Happy, Wealthy and United Country by 2050."[16] The mission is: "We will mobilize our people to create wealth through smart innovative ideas, quality services and equitable distribution of benefits."[17] In that pursuit the values are identified as "Integrity, Maturity, Diversity and Win-Win Relationships."[18] Out of the vision and mission statements flow five core areas with objectives and expected outcomes. These are first, sound and clear development plans; second, appropriate political and effective service delivery systems; third, best and productive human resource; fourth, dynamic and competitive economy; and fifth, happy and united country.

This document's background looks at the last thirty years of PNG as an independent country and the Eight Point Plan developed by its founders and concludes that "we have failed miserably in every one of the eight aims."[19] The way forward requires a "major transformation in the way we think, interact with one

---

16. PNG Institute of Public Administration, *Papua New Guinea National Strategic Plan 2010—2050*, final report to the National Development Summit (September 4, 2008) 7.

17. Ibid.

18. Ibid., 8.

19. Ibid., 2.

another and do business in the future.... To succeed we need a major shift in the mindset."[20] This is not a small task. Although this document does not deal with youth ministry, it does call for religious programs supporting the National Strategic Plan. Women are specifically mentioned several times in the document, but not youth. Perhaps this is because youth has its own strategic plan in place.[21] However, for a country where the median age is twenty[22], and about 40 percent of the total population are under the age of fifteen[23], this is a gross omission. Perhaps it is an indicator of what is to be expected in the future—even more segregation between adults and youth.

One thing is certain—a paradigm shift is needed. This also applies to the church and its work with youth. The church needs to think carefully what approach to take in working with and for the young population of PNG and young members of today's churches. Youth will need the help of adults to rediscover the beauty of their own country, their own skills, and their own life. It will require a leap of faith in each other and God. Both adults and youth will have to make a clear-cut decision whom they will follow, God from the Bible, or the spiritual world of their ancestors—the world that Western media portrays, or the example Jesus set.

There are some young people who are fully committed to God, as well as highly educated and well-situated in the business world of PNG. They will be role models for others to follow and their influence will be significant. PNG needs more such young people.

Damaro pointed out that whatever is happening in the West is coming to PNG or is already there. Thus PNG leaders need to find out what is happening in the West, as this is the trend that PNG is following. Society is fragmenting, and the church needs to

20. Ibid., 5.
21. See *National Youth Policy*.
22. Australian Bureau of Statistics, "3201.0 - Population by Age and Sex, Australian States and Territories, Jun 2010," accessed October 6, 201⁻, online: http://www.abs.gov.au/Ausstats/abs@.nsf/mf/3201.0.
23. AusAID, "About Papua New Guinea," accessed October 6, 201⁻, online: http://www.ausaid.gov.au/country/png/png_intro.cfm.

Part 2: Youth Ministry as Practical Theology in the SDA Context

be the unifying force in the new setup. Church needs to have the feel of a family, where young people will be welcomed, accepted, supported, and encouraged. It needs to open its doors to single families, AIDS sufferers, orphans, rascals, prostitutes, and prisoners, pointing the way to Christ, in whom all are one family.

In the part 2 of this book, youth ministry as practical theology was addressed by looking at several issues. It was seen that the Adventist view of eschatology greatly influences how and what kind of work with youth is done. It was pointed out that materials, ideas, and programs are exported from America and in that way influence people in their thinking and their creation of programs. Since the church originated in America, governance based on that style was also adopted in other parts of the world.

To better understand practical youth ministry, the history of youth ministry was presented both in the SDA Church at large and more specifically in PNG. Major contributors to that ministry were recognized, like Hugh Dickins and Kelvin Silva. Significant projects and developments were acknowledged.

The last point of interest in this part of the book was anticipated trends. Those that seem to be impacting the SDA Church as a whole were looked at first, and then specifically issues facing PNG. A time of big challenges and great opportunities is ahead.

This is the end of the background studies which need to be taken into consideration in order to craft a curriculum for a master's-level Introduction to Youth Ministry course in PNG. Next is the succinct curriculum, with course goals, learning outcomes, and elements of the curriculum. These will be the topics of the last part of this book.

PART 3

Curriculum for Introduction to Youth Ministry Course

CHAPTER 7

Course Goals and Learning Outcomes

THE MAIN POINTS OF discussion in this chapter are what an Introduction to Youth Ministry course should be anticipated to achieve and what benefit it will bring to the students and the society they will influence after they have completed the course. These are called course goals and learning outcomes. Before these are identified, however, it would be helpful to know who the students for this class will be and how that will affect the development of goals and learning outcomes.

The students who will be taking this course will already have completed a BA degree that has enabled them to work as pastors. They will have spent a few or many years pastoring several churches at once. These will be both male and female, although mostly male. Most, if not all, will be church-sponsored adult students. First, therefore, a look at adult learning is necessary.

When testing Kolb's Learning Style Inventory in PNG, Arden G. Sanders found several points about Kamasau, one of the people groups there. They believe that "learning should be by trial-error, and that it should be context-specific." They also "prefer their trainers to be persons whom they respect, and with whom they have an ongoing relationship. . . . They will function better if they are informed of the objectives for the training at the beginning, so they can put their training activities into the total context." They

Part 3: Curriculum for Introduction to Youth Ministry Course

prefer learning skills by "trying it out for themselves... rather than by listening to lectures." Finally, they "should be encouraged to work in groups and assist each other in study and assignments."[1] Although this was specifically for translators of the Bible in PNG, it highlights in particular the Melanesian context and it is not unlike what Malcolm S. Knowles describes. When he compares pedagogy and andragogy, he says that "an andragogical learning situation... is alive with meetings of small groups—planning committees, learning-teaching teams, consultation groups, project task forces—sharing responsibility for helping one another learn."[2]

According to Rosemary S. Caffarella, and several other authors before her, there are five main purposes for adult education. First, "to encourage continuous growth and development of individuals." Second, "to assist people in responding to practical problems and issues of adult life." Third, "to prepare people for current and future work opportunities." Fourth, "to assist organizations in achieving desired results and adapting to change." And fifth, "to provide opportunities to examine community and societal issues, foster change for the common good, and promote a civil society."[3] With developing this course in PNG, all five of these purposes should be kept in mind. The following paragraphs will show how these purposes will be achieved in this course.

First, the students are already willing to grow and develop, since they are studying to obtain a master's degree, but the course will help them to grow more and develop further. Second, by learning about youth ministry they will attempt to respond to practical issues they face in that ministry. The course will also open ways to address issues they face personally and organizationally. Third, those already involved in youth work will immediately benefit from this course. Some of them may not be involved in work with youth, and this course will help them appreciate its opportunities and problems. Pastors often move from one place to another, and having attended this course would prepare them

1. Sanders, "Learning," 202–8.
2. Knowles, *Modern*, 49.
3. Caffarella, *Planning*, 10.

Course Goals and Learning Outcomes

for potential future work. Fourth, since they belong to an organization—the church—they will help the church achieve desired results and adapt to the dramatic changes that are visible in PNG. Those that may be involved in administration of the church will find the course beneficial when influencing committees in their decision making. Finally, fifth, this course will help them examine diverse community and societal issues specific to PNG, and also worldwide. The Adventist Church and its programs are held in high esteem in PNG. Attending this course, and putting into practice what is learned will help continue that trend. Having considered the purpose of adult learning, a look at how adults learn is now necessary.

Adult learning differs from child learning because the self-concept of adults moves toward a "self-directing human being," they have much more experience in life from which to learn and keep on learning, they need to apply their knowledge immediately, and they learn because they want to learn—their motivation is internal.[4] On the other hand, their learning fits in with general orientations to theories of learning such as the behaviorist, cognitivist, humanist, social learning, and constructivist.[5] Each looks at learning from a different perspective. For example, the purpose of education in a behaviorist theory is to "produce behavioural change in desired direction," while for the humanist it is to "become self-actualized, autonomous."[6]

Marlene D. LeFever, in trying to help Sunday school teachers, used Bernice McCarthy's 4MAT System of four learning styles. She sees learners as imaginative, analytic, common sense, and dynamic. Each lesson should include all four styles in order to enable each student to participate in the whole lesson, to give them opportunity to show their strengths, and to develop them further, because each of the learners is asking a different question,

---

4. Merriam and Cafarella describe these theories and offer a helpful table with their summaries. Merriam and Caffarella, *Learning*, 272.

5. Ibid., 264.

6. Ibid.

Part 3: Curriculum for Introduction to Youth Ministry Course

as shown below.[7] Those whose learning style is imaginative look for meaning; they like to know why they need to know what is presented. The analytic ones are interested in content of the presentation; they want to grow in knowledge. The group belonging to common sense learning style like to experiment to find out how what is explained works in practice, while those whose learning style is dynamic are looking for creative application. They like to see what this can become. With this background of the purposes of learning in adulthood and explanation of how adults learn, course goals, and learning outcomes for Introduction to Youth Ministry, a master's-level course in PNG will be proposed.

Course Goals

Thinking through course goals "is one of the most difficult tasks people who plan programs do."[8] Often the term goals and objectives are understood differently. Some consider one to be specific and the other a broad statement of intent, while others believe it vice versa. In this book, goals are considered broad statements of intended achievement in a particular educational program, while learning outcomes will be specific statements, expressed as end results of the course.

The main goal of this course is to equip the students for the task of working with youth. This statement should be understood not as a definitive mark of attainment but that by completing this course, students will have enough learning experience to work in youth ministry and be stimulated for continuous growth in this area. It would be impossible that an Introduction to Youth Ministry course would equip the students in such a way that they do not need further skills or knowledge, especially in today's changing world. From this main goal several others are derived.

The goals listed here are not ordered and have equal importance. One, to have an appreciation of different worldviews

---

7. LeFever, *Learning*, 25.
8. Caffarella, *Planning*, 156.

Course Goals and Learning Outcomes

influencing today's PNG youth—traditional PNG culture mixed with occultism and Western media influence. Two, to be acquainted with issues youth are facing in the fast-changing world. Three, to understand the biblical foundations and mission for youth ministry. Four, to be acquainted with the history of youth ministry in the SDA Church, both in the church at large and in PNG. Five, while anticipating trends in society and the church, to develop ideas and plans for positively influencing youth in their area of work. Six, to research, analyze, and formulate strategies for creating and maintaining youth ministries that are culturally meaningful and biblically authentic.

Learning Outcomes

Learning outcomes are "clear statements of the anticipated results to be achieved through education and training programs."[9] They can be divided into several areas. Although L. Dee Fink acknowledges Bloom's well-known taxonomy of educational objectives, he proposes a new one that is based on change and not in the cognitive domain only. He classifies them in the "taxonomy of significant learning" as foundational knowledge, application, integration, human dimension, caring, and learning how to learn.[10] Since this course is envisaged as significant learning experience, Fink's construct will be followed.

"Foundational knowledge provides the basic understanding" of "science, history, literature, geography . . . major ideas and perspectives" in general terms.[11] By the end of the Introduction to Youth Ministry course the students will be acquainted with the history of youth ministry in the SDA Church. They will understand psychosocial stages in youth development from a Melanesian and Western perspective. They will know the biblical texts and concepts relating to family and youth. Students will be familiar with

---

9. Caffarella, *Planning*, 156.
10. Fink, *Creating*, 30–33.
11. Ibid., 31, 36–38.

Part 3: Curriculum for Introduction to Youth Ministry Course

the context in which youth ministry happens and its influences and ecology. They will be familiar with writers who significantly impacted youth ministry.

"Application learning" is "learning how to engage in various kinds of thinking [like] critical, creative, and practical," but "also includes developing certain skills [like] communication . . . or learning how to manage complex projects."[12] When this course is completed, the students will be able to formulate a framework for understanding the theological basis for youth ministry. They will freely communicate with each other about issues connected with youth ministry. They will be skilled in managing production and delivery of oral and written presentations on youth ministry topics.

"Integration" happens when "students are able to see and understand the connections between different things . . . [like] connections between specific ideas . . . people or between different realms of life."[13] By the end of the course, students will understand the connection between developmental stages of youth development and their faith development, reasoning, influences in society, and how that affects their behavior. They will also understand how the history of Western SDA youth ministry is connected with the history of the PNG youth ministry in their particular workplace. Further, they will better understand themselves and their attitudes toward old and young, their work in the past, and what is needed today.

"Human dimension" in significant learning experience is "when students learn something important about themselves or about others . . . [that] enables them to function and interact more effectively."[14] By the end of this course, students will have a better understanding of themselves, the context they come from, and influences on their life. They will better understand other students in the class and their backgrounds and reasons for their views. Consequently, they will better understand why youth act the way they do and how they can interact more effectively with them.

12. Ibid., 38–42.
13. Ibid., 42–44.
14. Ibid., 44–48.

Course Goals and Learning Outcomes

"Caring" means that "learning experience changes the degree to which students care about something . . . to a greater degree than they did before or in a different way." Because of that, they will "have the *energy* they need for learning more about it and making it part of their lives."[15] At the end of this course, students will be excited about youth ministry. They will develop curiosity about youth culture and a willingness to learn more about them in order to serve them better as leaders. Through this course they will develop appreciation for others who have worked in this field before them.

"Learning how to learn" is also a "process of learning itself," helping the students "to be a better student . . . engage in a particular kind of inquiry . . . become a self-directing learner." This will enable students to "*continue* learning in the future and to do so with *greater effectiveness*."[16] At the end of this course, students will be acquainted with different methods of learning and identify which is their favorite way of learning, together with how they can develop other areas. They will understand various elements of youth ministry from different perspectives both by reading from books and by conversations and tutorials in the class. They will have further developed their reading skills and critical thinking capabilities.

This chapter identified the major course goal of equipping the students for the task of working with youth, and several other goals that help clarify the major goal. Further, based on Fink's *Creating Significant Learning Experiences*, learning outcomes for the course were outlined. They are in the area of foundational knowledge, application, integration, human dimension, caring, and learning how to learn. The next chapter will further elaborate these topics in the elements of the curriculum as units, and also assignments and exams.

---

15. Ibid., 32, 48–49.
16. Ibid., 49–55 (italics in orginal).

CHAPTER 8

Elements of the Curriculum

CHAPTER 8 WILL PROVIDE elements of the curriculum. They will be divided into three subsections. The first one will describe the major units of the course. The second will explain the assignments required from the students. And the third will explain the instruments of measuring their performance.

Units

This course will be divided into five major units. It is envisaged that they will be completed in the order presented. Each unit may take different amounts of lecture time, as this will depend on the need and interest of students, which is difficult to ascertain prior to the course. A level of flexibility is therefore needed by the lecturer. The five major units after the introduction to the subject are: psychosocial and spiritual development of youth, environmental influences on youth, history of youth ministry, theology of youth ministry, and models of youth ministry. They are briefly described below.

Introduction

Introductory time spent with students will be used to establish several outcomes. Each student hopes to achieve specific goals while

Elements of the Curriculum

attending this course. These goals can be identified while the lecturer presents the outline of what he or she expects to offer students in the course, as well as the achievement expected from the students. It is envisaged that a learning-styles inventory will be conducted during the introduction to help the lecturer assess how to do the presentations and to help students in the learning process.

Psychosocial and Spiritual Development of Youth

From boy to man and girl to woman, a person goes through several developmental changes. Some are culturally based, some biologically universal. These in turn influence youth spirituality.

This unit needs to cover the psychosocial development of youth from a Melanesian perspective. Much discovery would be gained in group discussions and open sharing by students on the topic. It is anticipated that many different accounts would be gained, and perhaps even some consensus on what the stages of psychosocial development in PNG are. Recommended readings for this topic would be from Margaret Mead, Helen Sheils Fenbury, Paulias Matane, Gilbert Herdt, Ann Chowning, H. Ian Hogbin, Franco Zocca and Nicholas de Groot, Patricia K. Townsend, Jeline Giris, and Teresia Rynkiewich.[1]

It is important that students are also acquainted with the Western stages of psychosocial development. The starting point would be the changes to society brought by industrialization and the beginnings of study of adolescence. An overview of contributors to disciplines studying development, such as Erik Erikson, Jean Piaget, and Lawrence Kohlberg, is needed. More recent authors like Jeffrey J. Arnett and John W. Santrock would be required reading for this part of the course.

Connected to the psychosocial development, and perhaps of more interest to the student, is the spiritual development of children and youth. However, faith development is closely related to

---

1. Full bibliographical references for the authors mentioned are in the bibliography. Throughout this chapter, if the authors are not already mentioned in the bibliography, full bibliographical reference will be given in the footnote.

Part 3: Curriculum for Introduction to Youth Ministry Course

psychosocial development. The two main theories of faith development come from James W. Fowler and John H. Westerhoff III.[2] They can be related to motor-sensory, cognitive, and moral development that is covered in previous parts of psychosocial development. A helpful compilation from Eugene C. Roehlkepartain and others is *The Handbook of Spiritual Development in Childhood and Adolescence*.[3] Three emphases on spirituality to explore are spiritual disciplines which are based on individual spirituality, spirituality in community, and spirituality that is expressed in daily living through social justice.[4]

Environmental Influences on Youth

This unit will look at how family, peers, media, *wantok* system, animism, and education influence youth. These are influences present in the country; therefore, this topic will mainly be discussed from a PNG perspective. On the other hand, since media, especially through radio, television, internet, social media, and movies available for viewing on DVDs are largely coming from the West, this aspect will be looked at, as well. Animism will also be discussed at length, as it seems to be the foundation of all other environmental influences. Much of the material for this part will be easily discovered through class discussions; however, several authors are recommended for more data information and different opinions. Such sources are Blair Tindal, Asian Development Bank's articles on the Internet, Nathan Kwasam, Paulias Matane, *National Youth Policy of Papua New Guinea, 2007–2017*, Anne Dickson-Waiko, Vanessa Griffen, Moshe Rapaport, *The State of Pacific Youth*

---

2. James W. Fowler, *Stages of Faith: Psychology of Human Development and the Quest for Meaning* (San Francisco: Harper & Row, 1981); John H. Westerhoff III, *Will Our Children Have Faith?* (Harrisburg, PA: Morehouse, 2000).

3. Eugene C. Roehlkepartain et al., eds., *The Handbook of Spiritual Development in Childhood and Adolescence* (Thousand Oaks, CA: SAGE, 2006).

4. Suggested reading from Dallas Willard, *The Divine Conspiracy: Rediscovering Our Hidden Life in God* (San Francisco: Harper Collins, 1998); and John Drane, *Do Christians Know How to Be Spiritual? The Rise of New Spirituality and the Mission of the Church* (London: Darton, Longman & Todd, 2005).

Elements of the Curriculum

Report 2005, Daniel Shaw, Ennio Mantovani, Darrell Whiteman, and Neville Bartle for perspectives from PNG, and Chap Clark and David Elkind for the Western perspective.

Theology of Youth Ministry

There is a need for "something solid and deep on which to stand with young people, a way to move beyond the consumer habits and entertainment focus that too often consume youth ministry."[5] That need is theology, to be theologically grounded when dealing with youth. Biblical texts and concepts that deal with youth will be explored in this unit. Old and New Testament stories are simple and clear ways of seeing God's view of youth and youth's connection with God. Powerful concepts can be extracted and easily understood from these biblical accounts by the students for whom this is the best way of learning, since storytelling is one of the main ways they pass on knowledge in their oral culture. Further, terms used in the Bible for family and youth, both in the original Hebrew and Greek, will be helpful and will also be easily understood, since the students have had basic Hebrew and Greek studies in their undergraduate courses. Scriptures of special interest are Deuteronomy 6:2-7, John 13:34, Romans 8:23, Matthew 19:14, Matthew 18:4-6, 2 Timothy 3:16-17, and Galatians 5:5. Issues that are of particular importance to youth, some of which are sex, discernment, God, and hope, will be discussed here as grounded in the Bible and in Jesus. Recommended readings for this part of the course are from Kenda Creasy Dean, Andrew Root, Kevin J. Vanhoozer, and Ray Anderson.[6]

---

5. Root and Dean, *Theological*, 16.

6. Kevin J. Vanhoozer et al., eds., *Everyday Theology: How to Read Cultural Texts and Interpret Trends* (Grand Rapids: Baker Academic, 2007); Ray S. Anderson, *Shape of Practical Theology: Empowering Ministry with Theological Praxis* (Downers Grove, IL: InterVarsity, 2001).

Part 3: Curriculum for Introduction to Youth Ministry Course

History of Youth Ministry

Youth Ministry is 120 years old. There is much one can learn from those years. This unit will look at the beginnings of youth ministry in the world and its spread around world. Then the focus will move to youth ministry in the SDA Church from its beginnings in America to how it spread across the world. The final portion of this unit will narrow down youth ministry even further to its establishment and progress in PNG. This topic, the history of youth ministry in PNG, could eventually become someone's doctoral dissertation topic, as much information could be gathered through interviews with still-living pioneers of this work in PNG. It will be shown that Pathfinders and schools were the main avenues for youth work. Recommended reading for this section are from Richard W. Schwarz and Floyd Greenleaf, Thelma Silva, *Australasian Record*, and Robert Holbrook.[7]

Models of Youth Ministry

This unit will explore different models of youth ministry present in Western countries, with the aim that students will reflect on these and, in dialogue with each other, attempt to propose methods that could be used in their own settings. For this purpose they will need to reflect on the specifics of their environment and the developmental stages of youth in PNG. This will include discussions on the various issues of program-centered versus people-centered approach, purpose driven and family oriented and ministry for youth in or out of church. Recommended readings for this unit are from Doug Fields, Mark Yaconelli, Mark DeVries, Merton P. Strommen, and Richard A. Hardel.[8]

    7. Holbrook, *Pathfinder Story* (Washington, DC: GC Youth Ministry, 2006).
    8. Doug Fields, *Purpose-Driven Youth Ministry: 9 Essential Foundations for Healthy Growth* (Grand Rapids: Zondervan, 1998); Mark Yaconelli, *Contemplative Youth Ministry: Practicing the Presence of Jesus* (Grand Rapids: Zondervan, 2006); Mark DeVries, *Family-Based Youth Ministry: Reaching the Been-There, Done-That Generation* (Downers Grove, IL: InterVarsity, 1994); Merton P. Strommen and Richard A. Hardel, *Passing On the Faith: A Radical*

Assignments

Assignments in this course are designed to assist students in learning. S. D. Brookfield notes that assignments need to have three main ingredients. They should help students be more adept and critically reflective, they should assist them in developing their own learning habits, and should assist them in nurturing their self-confidence, opening ways to do things they did not deem possible earlier.[9]

Reading Report

In order for students to gain the most benefit from this course, it is important that they read selected materials in advance. Each student is required to read six hundred pages from the selected bibliography for this subject.[10] For each book or article, a reading report is to be written, up to two pages each, reflecting on the reading material, highlighting new ideas and how they could be used in the field of work the student is involved in. These reading reports are to be submitted at the beginning of classes. This will constitute 20 percent of their total marks.

Research Paper

Ellen White wrote that "no living man should be relied upon to think for us. No matter who it is, or what position he may be placed, we are not to look upon any man as a perfect criterion for us."[11] This was wise advice written over a hundred years ago to Seventh-day Adventists of the time. It is still valid today. One of the best ways to clarify one's thoughts is to write them down in an organized manner, hence the requirement for a research paper.

New Model for Youth and Family Ministry (Winona, MN: Saint Mary's, 2000).

9. Adapted from Brookfield, "Giving," 22, as quoted in Caffarela, *Planning*, 190.

10. Selected bibliography for this course is found in the appendix A.

11. White, *Counsels*, 44–45.

Part 3: Curriculum for Introduction to Youth Ministry Course

Students will be required to submit a fifteen- to twenty-page research paper they will write during the course and complete no later than two weeks after the course. The circumstances where these students live will make it extremely difficult to engage in further research after they have left the premises where this course will be held. Therefore the time given to submit this paper is short, helping them complete the bulk of it while attending the course. The paper will have three parts to it.

Part 1 is a report on an interview with a church member or members about youth ministry past and present. During the course there will be several opportunities to contact such a person or persons to conduct the interview; however, the interview could be conducted prior to attending class, as well. Part 2 is a brief reflection of current writings about practical youth ministry. Prior to attending classes, students will be expected to have read the required readings from which they can draw materials for this portion of the paper. In addition to prior reading, they will have available several online libraries to complement their reading while attending the course. Part 3 is a proposition on how to address the particular situation the student is currently working in, based on the first two parts of their paper. This assignment will constitute 40 percent of the total marks for this subject.

Journal

"The rationale for using reflective journaling in higher education is grounded in general learning theory, adult learning theory, experiential learning theory, and in the importance of the counselling student's personal growth and professional development."[12] Delaura L. Hubbs and Charles F. Brand further note that it is particularly suited for adult learners and highlight benefits of using reflective journaling in their education.

For three months prior to attending this course, each student will write a journal. They will record experiences they had with

---

12. Hubbs and Brand, "Paper Mirror," 60–71.

Elements of the Curriculum

youth, whether they perceived them to be positive or negative encounters. Journal entries need to be reflective and contain the following parts. Part 1 is a brief statement of what happened. Part 2 gives a comment on the experience—how it affected the student. Part 3 describes steps forward—what needs of youth this encounter highlighted? What solutions for youth emerged? How this helps the student in their youth ministry?

The third part of this journaling can be completed while reading for this course or during the course. It would be acceptable to submit this assignment readably handwritten. It should be submitted during the last period of classes. This assignment will be weighted at 20 percent of the total marks for this subject.

Group Presentation

There are many benefits of using student presentation as a learning tool. Brenda H. Spenser and Kathryn Bartle-Angus state that "students are able to work from their individual strengths . . . take responsibility for their own learning." Because they work in groups, they can see issues "from a variety of perspectives." It increases their "motivation and interest in the class" and it "creates an authentic learning environment."[13]

For this assignment, students will be divided into groups, based on their learning styles, preferably a representative of one in each group. Together they will prepare a presentation on a selected topic. The topic will be based on their journals, dealing with problems they have encountered. As a group they will research that problem to understand it better and to see how others may have addressed that issue. They will also need to search the Scriptures to find possible answers there. Finally, they will need to propose how that problem could be solved or at least addressed in their setting. After the presentation they will reflect on the process of doing this assignment. They will need to outline benefits and/or problems they experienced in producing the presentation and submit a brief reflection to the

13. Spenser and Bartle-Angus, "Presentation," 182–94.

Part 3: Curriculum for Introduction to Youth Ministry Course

lecturer. They will also prepare an outline of their presentation, to be used by other students during the presentation, which should be submitted to the lecturer through e-mail a day before their presentation is due, allowing the lecturer sufficient time for distribution. In the course outline, the explanation of this assignment will be done in point form to make it easier for students to see what is involved in the assignment and which steps to take. This assignment will be weighted at 20 percent of the total marks for the class.

Exams

There are different ways of ascertaining whether learning has happened in the course of study or not. Midterm and final exams are one such method. It is the writer's opinion that adequate learning will happen prior to and during this course, as well as through the required assignments. There will be no examination in this course apart from the assignments as outlined previously.

Elements of the curriculum were the topics discussed in this chapter. The two main parts were units and assignments. It is envisaged that five main units, after the introduction, will cover what is needed for a master's-level subject Introduction to Youth Ministry in PNG. The major units are Psychosocial and Spiritual Development of Youth, Environmental Influences on Youth, Theology of Youth Ministry, History of Youth Ministry, and Models of Youth Ministry. The course will require several assignments from students, some to be completed prior to attending the course and some during the course, with the possibility of having additional work afterward. The assignments are a reading report, a research paper, a journal, and a group presentation. With these requirements fulfilled there will be no need for an examination.

In the remaining part of this book, a summary and conclusion are presented. Following the summary there are appendices with selected bibliography and sample lesson plans for this course. At the end there is a list of references cited in the book.

Summary and Conclusion

THE PURPOSE OF THIS book was to present a curriculum for a master's-level Introduction to Youth Ministry course that is biblically based and contextually relevant for PNG pastors and youth workers. This book dealt with this topic in three major sections. The first part presented the challenge of youth ministry in PNG by discussing three main issues: context, psychosocial development, and influences and ecology.

Chapter 1 described the context of PNG society based on the area in which a citizen might live. It was seen that whether a person grew up in a village or city, island or the Highlands, will have a great impact on their worldview, habits, language, and even personal features. Traditions may be completely opposite in different parts of PNG. Pastors working with youth in different parts of PNG will need to learn the local context and should not assume that they understand the culture without investigation. The challenge is bigger when such pastors live in the place where several cultures meet and mix.

Chapter 2 identified the psychosocial development of youth as seen in Melanesian cultures and also described in Western societies. It pointed out the characteristics of both and the changes that are occurring in both views. What can be said for certain is that there are differences in how development is seen in the diverse cultures of PNG. Physical changes in a child are more important in this culture than age. Initiation rites are still practiced in many parts of PNG, while they are almost nonexistent in the Western world.

Summary and Conclusion

Chapter 3 addressed influences on the youth of PNG. It described media influences such as radio, television, music, the Internet, and print. It pointed out the rapid changes in society brought through the recent "invasion" of Western media. It also looked at the influence of family, both immediate, extended, and *wantok* system, and the role that animistic background plays. Family is very important, both immediate and extended. Decisions are made, like approval for marriage, in consultation with family members. Cousins are considered brothers and sisters, and only further questioning will reveal that they are not of the same mother and father. Life in Melanesia is not compartmentalized as is in the West, and binding it all together is the animistic belief system.

The second part of this book discussed youth ministry as practical theology in the SDA context. This part gave an overview of practical theology, the history of youth ministry, and anticipated trends in the practice of youth ministry in its three chapters. Chapter 4 assessed the biblical call of adoption and practical theology. It provided an overview of the biblical view of family and youth ministry, drawing from Old and New Testaments. It looked at different stories in the Bible but also specific terms used for family and youth to better understand biblical concepts. It called the church to be a family-like community, especially for youth in the cities. The second part of this chapter identified the most significant and distinctive aspects of Adventism to see how they influenced the approach to practical ministry with youth. This was limited to the SDA view of eschatology, the roots of Adventism based in the United States and as such transported to other parts of the world, and the type of governance of the church. The SDA view of eschatology gives youth ministry the urgency of work needed to be completed. Many concepts and methods to do so were exported from the United States, which was sometimes helpful, sometimes unhelpful. The same could be said about the system of governance in the church. It was exported from America, and it was helping the mission of the church in the beginning, but today there is a feeling that this system is hindering the work.

Summary and Conclusion

Chapter 5 briefly discussed the history of youth ministry in the SDA Church. It looked at the general development of youth ministry as originating in the United States. The need to work with youth and help youth in their growth was noticed by James White much earlier than the church was officially organized. The beginnings of what resembled official youth ministry, as could be recognized today, is attributed to two teenagers. By now the SDA Church has fully developed programs for working with young through its Sabbath School program and, separate from that, its Adventurers, Pathfinders, and Ambassadors programs. This chapter then portrayed the same process in the PNG setting. It was transported to PNG with some adaptations to suit the local context.

Chapter 6 looked at the anticipated trends in youth ministry in the SDA Church and their possible impact in PNG. The chapter was divided into two parts, one looking at the SDA Church in general and the other specifically at the PNG setting. It outlined problems and opportunities in both settings. In today's global village atmosphere, many issues are the same, although they may manifest themselves in different ways in different settings. It is a time of great opportunities to make a difference in young people's lives. And a time when young people can make a significant positive impact in the society.

The third part of this book offered a suggested curriculum for a master's-level Introduction to Youth Ministry course in PNG. Two chapters covered course goals with learning outcomes and elements of the curriculum. Chapter 7 proposed the course goals and learning outcomes for the course. It is specific for the PNG setting, substantially based on the information provided in part 1 and 2 of this document. The main goal for this course is to equip the students for the task of working with youth. From this main goal, six other goals were outlined. After the goals, learning outcomes were described, following Dee Fink's classification of significant learning as foundational knowledge, application, integration, human dimension, caring, and learning how to learn.

Summary and Conclusion

Chapter 8 provided elements of the curriculum. It gave information on the major units of the course. These are psychosocial and spiritual development of youth, environmental influences on youth, history of youth ministry, theology of youth ministry, and models of youth ministry. This chapter presented an explanation of the assignments required from the students. Four main assignments were proposed: a reading report, a research paper, a journal, and a group presentation. These are considered instruments of measuring an individual student's performance and no additional examinations are deemed necessary.

Following this summary and conclusion are appendices A and B. Appendix A has a selected bibliography of required reading for this course. Appendix B contains sample lesson plans for each of the major units of the course. After the appendices, the bibliography is found, which contains only the cited works. Many other books and articles pertaining to youth ministry could have been added, as they were consulted for this book, but since they were not quoted, they are not included.

Pastors need to be equipped for the task of working with youth who are confronted with changes. They need to learn from the knowledge about dealing with youth in the Western countries, since the same issues are affecting PNG youth. They need to also take into account the local circumstances that are specific to the youth of PNG. They need to base their plans and programs on sound biblical theology. Therefore, the purpose of this book was to present the curriculum for a master's-level Introduction to Youth Ministry course that is biblically based and contextually relevant for the PNG pastors and youth workers.

This book is, however, not limited to use by pastors working in youth ministry in PNG. Those working in the Solomon Islands can also benefit from these materials, because of similarities between the two cultures. Further still, it would be beneficial if SDA Church leaders, both in Melanesia and in the Sydney headquarters, use this book to help them understand the needs in PNG. Moreover, the work presented here can provide valuable insights to those involved in work where different cultures meet, especially

Summary and Conclusion

for those coming to Melanesia—business people, ambassadors, community workers, and health providers. It may be beneficial for educators in different parts of PNG, whether they are foreigners or locals from another part of the country.

This book can further be seen as a stepping stone for much-needed research in the area of youth in PNG. Both quantitative and qualitative research in youth culture in PNG is needed. Questions that need clarification are many, a few will suffice here. How many youth are in the church today as compared to ten years ago? What are the reasons that some have left the church and the others remained? What aspects of the programs offered now are meeting the needs of youth in the church, and what needs are not met? How many youth are committing suicide, both in the church and in the community at large? How is the AIDS epidemic affecting youth in the church?

For a while, the Papua New Guinea Tourism Promotion Authority[1] advertisement motto for PNG was "The Land of the Unexpected."[2] Of course they were alluding to the many mysteries and beauties beyond expectation that would be discovered by tourists. It was jokingly used in a negative way. When something went wrong, like electricity was off, a plane was delayed, or a car had a flat tire or ran out of petrol, people would comment, "The land of the unexpected." The lecturer who will be teaching this course will need to be flexible and prepared for unexpected things to happen. They need to have a "plan B" for every lecture. This is meant in both ways. Indeed, electricity may go off and PowerPoint presentations may not be shown, or that important video clip will have to wait for some other time. Nevertheless, the insights into culture, land, and beautiful people of PNG will far outweigh those inconveniences. A lecturer will return enriched beyond expectations.

---

1. The official website is www.pngtourism.org.pg (accessed December 1, 2011). The current motto is "A million different journeys."

2. Inserting this phrase into a Google search will yield many finds. The phrase is still commonly used. See the article by Hayward-Jones, "PNG."

Appendix A

Selected Bibliography for Introduction to Youth Ministry Course

Clark, Chap. *Hurt 2.0: Inside the World of Today's Teenagers.* Grand Rapids: Baker Academic, 2011.

Dean, Kenda Creasy, et al. *Starting Right: Thinking Theologically about Youth Ministry.* Grand Rapids: Zondervan, 2001.

Elkind, David. *All Grown Up and No Place to Go: Teenagers in Crisis.* Reading, MA: Addison-Wesley, 1984.

Fenbury, Helen Sheils, ed. *Childhood in Papua New Guinea: Personal Accounts of Growing Up in a Changing Society.* Goroka, PNG: Institute of Medical Research, 2009.

Hirsch, Eric. "Making Up People in Papua." *The Journal of the Royal Anthropological Institute* 7, no. 2 (June 2001) 241–56. Accessed October 17, 2010. Online: http://www.jstor.org/stable/2662112.

Holbrook, Robert, ed. *The AY Story: A Brief History of Youth Ministry in the Seventh-Day Adventist Church.* Collegedale, TN: College, 2005.

Mantovani, Ennio, ed. *An Introduction to Melanesian Religions: A Handbook for Church Workers.* Point Series 6. Goroka, PNG: Melanesian Institute, 1984.

Matane, Paulias. *My Childhood in New Guinea.* Melbourne: Oxford University Press, 1972.

Mundhenk, Kent. "Common Threads of Animism." *Melanesian Journal of Theology* 11, no. 1 (2006) 6–15.

National Youth Policy of Papua New Guinea 2007-2017. National Youth Commission of Papua New Guinea, 2007.

Root, Andrew, and Kenda Creasy Dean. *The Theological Turn in Youth Ministry.* Downers Grove, IL: IVP, 2011.

Santrock, John W. *Adolescence.* 8th ed. Boston: McGraw-Hill, 2001.

Selected Bibliography for Introduction to Youth Ministry Course

Silva, Thelma. "History of Youth Ministry in Papua New Guinea & the Solomon Islands." In *A Brief History of Youth Ministry in the South Pacific: Personal and Spiritual Growth*. Teaching resource for the Master Guide Program. Sydney: Seventh-day Adventist Church Youth Ministries of the South Pacific Division, 2010. Accessed May 15, 2013. Online: http://pathfinders.adventistconnect.org/site_data/86/assets/0025/1420/MG_SPD_History_of_Youth_Ministry_-_Apr_2010.pdf.

Townsend, Patricia K. *The Situation of Children in Papua New Guinea*. Waigani, PNG: Report prepared by the Papua New Guinea Institute of Applied Social and Economic Research for the Department of Finance and Planning, 1985.

Appendix B[1]

Sample Lesson Studies

[1]. This format is adopted from Caffarella, 194. The term used in the book is "Sample Instructional Plan."

Sample Lesson Studies

Sample Lesson Study				
Unit: Introduction		Title: Learning Styles	Time: 50 minutes	
Learning objectives: The students will be able to	Content Heading	Key Points to Emphasize	Instructional Techniques	Estimated Time
Identify four learning styles	Present four learning styles	Each person learns differently. There is no right or wrong. Each has benefits and limitations. Four basic learning styles: imaginative, analytic, common sense, dynamic.	PowerPoint Presentation	25 minutes
Analyze personal preference for learning	Answer questionnaire	Students answer questions individually to find their own preference for learning	Individual work using internet (or handout)	10 minutes
Consider benefits of other learning styles	Apply learning styles	Explain your learning style to the group. Each to comment on discovered benefits of other's learning style.	Small group discussion	15 minutes
Instructional resources and equipment needed:				
For Instructor			For Students	
Data projector, screen, power cord extension, PowerPoint Presentation, website address and handout questionnaire, in case there is no electricity or Internet connection.			Laptop Handout	

Sample Lesson Studies

Sample Lesson Study

Unit: Psychosocial and spiritual development of youth		Title: Melanesian view of psychosocial development	Time: 50 minutes	
Learning objectives: The students will be able to	Content Heading	Key Points to Emphasize	Instructional Techniques	Estimated Time
Identify Melanesian views of psychosocial development	Melanesian view of psychosocial development	Physical evidence of development, ages of children when this development is expected, societal responses to development or lack of it	Question and Answer Stories from different authors for illustration	20 minutes
Reflect on differences and similarities	Differences and similarities	Areas of PNG Similarities in views Differences in views	Discussion in two groups, one dealing with similarities, the other with differences	15 minutes
Make a classification for major areas of PNG	Classification	Areas of PNG Developmental stages Societal responses Ages	Small group discussion	15 minutes
Instructional resources and equipment needed:				
For Instructor			For Students	
Chart ready for distribution Stories from different authors for illustration			Chart for students to fill	

Sample Lesson Studies

Sample Lesson Study				
Unit: Environmental influences on youth	Title: Social Media and technology in the USA and PNG	Time: 50 minutes		
Learning objectives: The students will be able to	Content Heading	Key Points to Emphasize	Instructional Techniques	Estimated Time
Understand the importance of social media and technology for adolescents	Importance of social media and technology	Texting, social networking, gaming are important means to meet their relational needs and social belonging	Lecture with PowerPoint Presentation, YouTube video, Facebook, texting	35 minutes
Compare US situation with PNG	Comparison	Trend from USA is evident in PNG	Q&A time	15 minutes
Instructional resources and equipment needed:				
For Instructor		For Students		
Data projector, screen, power cord extension, PowerPoint Presentation, website address for YouTube, and Facebook account.		Laptop Open Facebook account if the student does not have one; send SMS text to a friend		

Sample Lesson Study

Unit: History of youth ministry	Title: History of youth ministry in the world	Time: 50 minutes		
Learning objectives: The students will be able to	Content Heading	Key Points to Emphasize	Instructional Techniques	Estimated Time
Name a selection of those who significantly impacted youth ministry	Youth ministry leaders	Youth leaders come from different parts of the world, however those considered significant may be coming from the USA	Internet search by small groups of students	10 minutes
Examine their contribution	Contribution of youth ministry leaders	They identified that youth need special attention in the church, they decided to use any necessary means to reach youth for Christ	Individual reading and report	30 minutes
Reflect on their impact today	Impact today	Disconnect between youth and adults	Lecture	10 minutes
Instructional resources and equipment needed:				
For Instructor			For Students	
Names of significant youth workers in the world, website address, in case there is no electricity or Internet connection, handout ready with information about several youth leaders and their contribution.			Laptop (handout)	

Sample Lesson Studies

Sample Lesson Study					
Unit: Theology of youth ministry		Title: Ellen G. White's view on youth ministry		Time: 50 minutes	
Learning objectives: The students will be able to	Content Heading	Key Points to Emphasize	Instructional Techniques		Estimated Time
Identify EGW's publications on youth	EGW's publications on youth	Historical background of her time EGW wrote about youth work in many publications over time Her last message was regarding youth	Lecture with power point presentation		15 minutes
Analyze EGW's ideas about youth work	EGW's writings on youth	Selected quotes from her writings point to the necessity of youth work, importance of youth, God's plan for youth, examples from the Bible that teach about how to do youth work	Individual work using handout with Internet search as a possibility to find other EGW writings		20 minutes
Synthesize EGW's view of youth ministry	EGW's view of youth ministry	EGW emphasized the importance of youth work	Small group discussion		15 minutes
Instructional resources and equipment needed:					
For Instructor			For Students		
Data projector, screen, power cord extension, PowerPoint Presentation, website address and handout with EGW's quotes.			Laptop Handout		

Sample Lesson Studies

Sample Lesson Study				
Unit: Models of youth ministry	Title: Purpose Driven Youth Ministry		Time: 50 minutes	
Learning objectives: The students will be able to	Content Heading	Key Points to Emphasize	Instructional Techniques	Estimated Time
Identify nine essential foundations for healthy growth	9 Foundations	The power of God, purpose, potential audience, programs, process, planned values, parents, participating leaders, perseverance	PowerPoint Presentation	35 minutes
Detect how these foundations correspond to youth work in PNG	9 Foundations and PNG	What is relevant for PNG setting, what could be adapted for PNG setting	Group discussion	15 minutes
Clarify the foundations	9 Foundations	Clarify requested point	Q&A	5 minutes
Instructional resources and equipment needed:				
For Instructor			For Students	
Data projector, screen, power cord extension, PowerPoint Presentation, book Purpose Driven Youth Ministry			Laptop	

Bibliography

Allen, Michael R. *Male Cults and Secret Initiations in Melanesia.* Melbourne: Melbourne University Press, 1967.
Arnett, Jeffrey J. *Adolescence and Emerging Adulthood: A Cultural Approach.* Upper Saddle River, NJ: Prentice Hall, 2004.
AusAID. *Pacific Economic Survey 2008.* Canberra, Australia: Australian Agency for International Development, 2008. Accessed May 15, 2011. Online: http://www.ausaid.gov.au/Publications/Documents/pacific_economic_survey08.pdf.
Bartle, Neville. *Death, Witchcraft and the Spirit World in the Highlands of Papua New Guinea: Developing a Contextual Theology in Melanesia.* Point Series 29. Goroka, PNG: Melanesian Institute, 2005.
Beaver, R. Pierce, et al., eds. *A Lion Handbook: The Word's Religions.* Oxford: Lion, 1982.
Berzonsky, Michael D. *Adolescent Development.* New York: Macmillan, 1981.
Brady, Ivan A., ed. *Transactions in Kinship, Adoption and Fosterage in Oceania.* Honolulu: University Press of Hawaii, 1976.
Brookfield, S. D. "Giving Helpful Evaluations to Learners." *Adult Learning* 3, no. 8 (1992) 22–24.
Brown, Francis. *The New Brown-Driver-Briggs-Gesenius Hebrew and English Lexicon.* Peabody, MA: Hendrickson, 1979.
Brown, William E. "Adoption." In *Baker Theological Dictionary of the Bible,* edited by Walter A. Elwell, 11–12. Grand Rapids: Baker, 1996.
Bruinsma, Reinder. "Present Truth Revisited: An Adventist Perspective on Postmodernism." Unpublished manuscript consulted by author in 2011.
Caffarella, Rosemary S. *Planning Programs for Adult Learners: A Practical Guide for Educators, Trainer, and Staff Developers.* 2nd ed. San Francisco: Jossey-Bass, 2002.
Campbell, I. J. "Savages with Whistling Arrows Live in Three-Storey Huts." *Australasian Record* 61, no. 10 (March 1957) 1.
Chowning, Ann. "Child Rearing and Socialization." In *Encyclopaedia of Papua New Guinea,* edited by Peter Ryan, 1:156–64. Melbourne: Melbourne University Press, 1972.

Bibliography

Clark, Chap. *Hurt: Inside the World of Today's Teenagers.* Grand Rapids: Baker Academic, 2004.

Clark, Chap, and Dee Clark. *Disconnected: Parenting Teens in a MySpace World.* Grand Rapids: Baker, 2007.

Commonwealth Secretariat. *Small States: Economic Review and Basic Statistics* 11. London: Commonwealth Secretariat, 2007.

Dean, Kenda Creasy, et al. *Starting Right: Thinking Theologically about Youth Ministry.* Grand Rapids: Zondervan, 2001.

"Department of Education: Anti-Social Student Subculture." Unpublished manuscript. Port Moresby, PNG: 2004.

Dickins, Hugh A. "Why Island Apostasies Are Few." *Australasian Record* 60, no. 47 (November 1956) 3.

Dickson-Waiko, Anne. "Polygamy, Social Safety Net or Cultural Anachronism? A Rejoinder." *South Pacific Journal of Philosophy and Culture* 7 (2003) 64–70.

Drawii, Judy Tatu. "Cult on the Rise? Students' Perspectives on Cult Issues in Secondary and National High Schools in Papua New Guinea." MA thesis, University of Waikato, 2008.

Elkind, David. *All Grown Up and No Place to Go: Teenagers in Crisis.* Reading, MA: Addison-Wesley, 1984.

———. *Hurried Child: Growing Up Too Fast Too Soon.* Reading, MA: Addison-Wesley, 1981.

Epstein, A. L. *Gunantuna: Aspects of the Person, the Self and the Individual among the Tolai.* Bathurst, Australia: Crawford House, 1999.

Erikson, Erik H. *Childhood and Society.* 2nd ed. New York: Norton, 1963.

———. "Memorandum on Youth." *Daedalus* 96, no. 3 (1967) 860–70. Accessed November 11, 2010. Online: http://www.jstor.org/stable/20027079.

Erickson, Matilda. *Missionary Volunteers and Their Work.* Washington, DC: Review and Herald, 1920.

Fenbury, Helen Sheils, ed. *Childhood in Papua New Guinea: Personal Accounts of Growing Up in a Changing Society.* Goroka, PNG: Institute of Medical Research, 2009.

Fink, L. Dee. *Creating Significant Learning Experiences: An Integrated Approach to Designing College Courses.* San Francisco: Jossey-Bass, 2003.

Freud, Sigmund. *Psychopathology of Everyday Life.* Translated by A. A. Brill. New York: Macmillan, 1916.

Garcia-Marenko, Alfredo. "Adventist Camporee Attracts 20,000 Pathfinders from 34 Countries." *Adventist World* 7, no. 7 (July 9, 2011) 6–7.

Giris, Jeline, and Teresia Rynkiewich. "Emerging Issues for Women and Children in Papua New Guinea." *Occasional Paper of Melanesian Institute*, no. 12 (2005) 1–30.

Goodson, Dale. "Evangelizing How? Project Scrapbook of Cultural Data." Unpublished teaching material prepared for MA course at Pacific Adventist University, Port Moresby, PNG, 2003.

Griffen, Vanessa. "Gender Relations in Pacific Cultures and Their Impact on the Growth and Development of Children." Paper prepared for UNICEF

seminar on Children's Rights and Culture in the Pacific, October 30, 2006. Accessed May 15, 2013. Online: http://www.unicef.org/eapro/Gender_Relations_in_Pacific_cultures.pdf.
Gustafsson, Berit. "Poverty and Informal Social Safety Nets in Papua New Guinea: A Literature Survey." The National Research Institute Special Publication 46 (2007) 7–41.
Guy, Richard. "Traditional and Non-traditional Mechanisms Designed to Alleviate Economic and Social Hardships on Wagiva Island, Milne Bay Province." The National Research Institute Special Publication 46 (2007) 42–74.
Harris, R. Laird, ed. *Theological Wordbook of the Old Testament*. Vol. 1. Chicago: Moody Press, 1980.
Hayward-Jones, Jenny. "PNG, Land of the Unexpected." *Intepreter*, August 3, 2011. Accessed December 1, 2011. Online: http://www.lowyinterpreter.org/post/2011/08/03/Papua-New-Guinea-land-of-the-unexpected.aspx.
Henry, Rosita. "'Smoke in the Hills, Gunfire in the Valley': War and Peace in Western Highlands, Papua New Guinea." *Oceania* 75, no. 4 (2005) 431–43.
Herdt, Gilbert, ed. *Rituals of Manhood: Male Initiation in Papua New Guinea*. Berkeley: University of California Press, 1982.
Hirsch, Eric. "Making Up People in Papua." *The Journal of the Royal Anthropological Institute* 7, no. 2 (June 2001) 241–56. Accessed October 17, 2010. Online: http://www.jstor.org/stable/2662112.
Hogbin, H. Ian. "A New Guinea Childhood: From Weaning till the Eighth Year in Wogeo." *Oceania* 16, no. 4 (1946) 275–96.
Holbrook, Robert, ed. *The AY Story: A Brief History of Youth Ministry in the Seventh-Day Adventist Church*. Collegedale, TN: College, 2005.
Hubbs, Delaura L., and Charles F. Brand. "The Paper Mirror: Understanding Reflective Journaling." *Journal of Experiential Education* 28, no. 1 (2005) 60–71. Accessed November 30, 2011. Online: http://www.questia.com/PM.qst?a=o&d=5035540466.
Jacka, Jerry. "Coca-Cola and *Kolo*: Land, Ancestors and Development." *Anthropology Today* 17, no. 4 (August 2001) 3–8. Accessed October 17, 2010. Online: http://www.jstor.org/stable/2678183.
Janssen, Hermann. "'Wantoks' Everywhere: Kinship and Christian Family Life in Young Churches." *Catalyst* 7, no. 4 (1977) 288–97.
Kellner, Mark A. "'Variance' for North American, Trans-European Division Constitutions Fails Annual Council Vote." *Adventist News Network*, October 12, 2011. Accessed May 15, 2013. Online: http://news.adventist.org/archive/articles/2011/10/12/variance-for-north-american-trans-european-division-constitutions-fails-ann.
Khambu, John. "Miruma Village, Eastern Highlands Province: A Social Safety Net Study." National Research Institute Special Publication 46 (2007) 62–72.
Knight, George R. *Anticipating the Advent*. Boise, ID: Pacific Press Publishing Association, 1992.

Bibliography

Knowles, Malcolm S. *The Modern Practice of Adult Education: From Pedagogy to Andragogy*. New York: Cambridge Adult Education, 1980.

Kwasam, Nathan. *The Internet and Effects on Papua New Guinea*. PNG: South Pacific Centre for Communication and Information in Development, University of Papua New Guinea. Accessed September 19, 2010. Online: http://www.pngbuai.com/600technology/information/waigani/InternetEffectsPNG/WaiSemNathan.pdf.

Lahari, Willie. "The Challenges of Measuring Community Access to Information and Communication Technologies (ICT) in Papua New Guinea." Paper by the deputy national statistician, Papua New Guinea, November 2004. Accessed September 16, 2010. Online: http://www.itu.int/ITU-D/ict/mexico04/doc/doc/30_png_e.pdf.

LeFever, Marlene D. *Learning Styles: Reaching Everyone God Gave You to Teach*. Colorado Springs, CO: David C. Cook, 1995.

Leh, Amy S. C., and Richard Kennedy. "Instructional and Information Technology in Papua New Guinea." *Educational Technology Research and Development* 52, no. 1 (2004) 96–101. Accessed September 19, 2010. Online: http://www.jstor.org/stable/30220380.

Lemke, E. C. "First Sepik Camp-Meeting." *Australasian Record* 60, no. 2 (January 9, 1956) 8–9.

Maher, Robert F. *New Men of Papua: A Study in Cultural Change*. Madison: University of Wisconsin Press, 1961.

Mantovani, Ennio, ed. *An Introduction to Melanesian Religions: A Handbook for Church Workers*. Point Series 6. Goroka, PNG: Melanesian Institute, 1984.

Marape, Warren. "PNGATSA Combined Worship." *Harina* 25, no. 3 (April 10, 2008) 1–4. Accessed November 20, 2011. Online: http://www.pau.ac.pg/assets/276862.

Matane, Paulias. *My Childhood in New Guinea*. Melbourne: Oxford University Press, 1972.

Matane, Paulias, and M. L. Ahuja. *Papua New Guinea: Land of Natural Beauty and Cultural Diversity*. New Delhi: CBS, 2005.

McConnell, James V. *Understanding Human Behaviour*. 5th ed. New York: Holt, Rinehart, and Winston, 1986.

Mead, Margaret. *Coming of Age in Samoa*. New York: Dell, 1928.

———. *Growing Up in New Guinea: A Study of Adolescence and Sex in Primitive Societies*. Harmondsworth, UK: Penguin, 1930.

Merriam, Sharan B., and Rosemary S. Caffarella. *Learning in Adulthood: A Comprehensive Guide*, 2nd ed. San Francisco: Jossey-Bass, 1999.

Misha, Timothy. "Case Study: The Impact of the Middle Sepik River People's Cultural Practices and Spirit-Worship on Their Christian Worship." *Melanesian Journal of Theology* 24, no. 1 (2008) 43–80.

Mantovani, Ennio, ed. *An Introduction to Melanesian Religions: A Handbook for Church Workers*. Point Series 6. Goroka, PNG: Melanesian Institute for Pastoral and Socio-Economic Service, 1984.

Bibliography

Mueller, Ivo, and Thomas A. Smith. "Patterns of Child Growth in Papua New Guinea and Their Relation to Environmental, Dietary and Socioeconomic Factors – Further Analyses of the 1982–1983 Papua New Guinea National Nutrition Survey." *Papua New Guinea Medical Journal* 42, no. 3–4 (1999) 94–113. Accessed November 30, 2010. Online: http://www.pngimr.org.pg/png_med_journal/Patterns%20%20-%20Sep_Dec%2099.pdf.

Mundhenk, Kent. "Common Threads of Animism." *Melanesian Journal of Theology* 11, no. 1 (2006) 6–15.

Muri, David. "Guard Chops PAU Female Student." *Post-Courier Online*, November 21, 2011. Accessed November 21, 2011. Online: http://www.postcourier.com.pg/20111121/news06.htm.

National Youth Policy of Papua New Guinea, 2007–2017. National Youth Commission of Papua New Guinea, 2007.

Oliver, Barry David. *SDA Organizational Structure: Past, Present and Future*. Andrews University Seminary Doctoral Dissertation Series 15. Berrien Springs, MI: Andrews University Press, 1989.

Partridge, Christopher, ed. *The New Lion Handbook: The World's Religions*. Oxford: Lion Hudson, 2005.

Piaget, Jean. *The Origins of Intelligence in Children*. Translated by Margaret Cook. New York: International Universities Press, 1952.

Rapaport, Moshe, ed. *The Pacific Islands: Environment & Society*. Honolulu: Bess, 1999.

Root, Andrew, and Kenda Creasy Dean. *The Theological Turn in Youth Ministry*. Downers Grove, IL: IVP, 2011.

Sanders, Arden Glenn. "Learning Styles in Melanesia: Toward the Use and Implications of Kolb's Model for National Translator Training." PhD diss., Fuller Theological Seminary, 1988.

Santrock, John W. *Adolescence*. 8th ed. Boston: McGraw-Hill, 2001.

Schubert, Branimir. "The Courage to Lead." *Leadership Roundtable* 8, no. 2 (July 2011) 8–12.

Schwarz, Richard W., and Floyd Greenleaf. *Light Bearers: A History of the Seventh-day Adventist Church*. Nampa, ID: Pacific Press Publishing Association, 1995.

Senn, Milton J. E., et al. "Insights on the Child Development Movement in the United States," *Monographs of the Society for Research in Child Development* 40, no. 3–4 (August 1975) 1–107.

Shaw, Daniel. "The Wantok System: Local Principles and Expatriate Perspective." *Catalyst* 11, no. 3 (1981) 190–203.

Silva, Thelma. "History of Youth Ministry in Papua New Guinea & the Solomon Islands." In *A Brief History of Youth Ministry in the South Pacific: Personal and Spiritual Growth*. Teaching resource for the Master Guide Program. Sydney: Seventh-day Adventist Church Youth Ministries of the South Pacific Division, 2010. Accessed May 15, 2013. Online: http://pathfinders.adventistconnect.org/site_data/86/assets/0025/1420/MG_SPD_History_of_Youth_Ministry_-_Apr_2010.pdf.

Bibliography

Spenser, Brenda H., and Kathryn Bartle-Angus. "The Presentation Assignment: Creating Learning Opportunities for Diverse Student Populations." *Journal of College Reading and Learning* 30, no. 2 (2000) 182–94. Accessed November 30, 2011. Online: http://www.questia.com/PM.qst?a=o&d=5001754798.

State of Pacific Youth 2005. Collaborative report by UNICEF Pacific; Secretariat of the Pacific Community, Noumea; and United Nations Population Fund (Office for the Pacific); funded by New Zealand's International Aid and Development Agency. Suva, Fiji: 2005.

Sternberg, Jason. "Young, Dumb and Full of Lies: the News Media's Construction of Youth Culture." *Australian Screen Education* 37 (2004) 34–39.

Tasker, David R. *Ancient Near Eastern Literature and the Hebrew Scriptures about the Fatherhood of God*. New York: Peter Lang, 2004.

Thayer, Joseph Henry. *The New Thayer's Greek-English Lexicon of the New Testament*. Peabody, MA: Hendrickson, 1981.

Thornburg, Hershel D. *Development in Adolescence*. Monterey, CA: Brooks/Cole, 1975.

Tindall, Blair. "Papua New Guinea." Media, TV, Radio, Newspapers. *Press Reference*. Accessed September 19, 2010. Online: http://www.pressreference.com/No-Sa/Papua-New-Guinea.html.

Townend, Calvyn A. *One Plus One Equals One: Ideas and Ideals for Pacific Families*. Warburton, Australia: Signs, 2000.

Townsend, Patricia K. *The Situation of Children in Papua New Guinea*. Waigani, PNG: Report prepared by the Papua New Guinea Institute of Applied Social and Economic Research for the Department of Finance and Planning, 1985.

Trompf, G. W. *Payback, the Logic of Retribution in Melanesian Religions*. Cambridge: Cambridge University Press, 1994.

Wallace, John M., Jr., and Jerald G. Bachman. "Explaining Racial/Ethnic Differences in Adolescent Drug Use: The Impact of Background and Lifestyle." *Social Problems* 38, no. 3 (1991) 333–57. Accessed November 17, 2010. Online: http://www.jstor.org/stable/800603.

Webb, Douglas. "An Assessment of Options for a Pacific Regional Telecommunications and ICT Resource Centre." Report commissioned by the Public-Private Infrastructure Advisory Service of the World Bank, December 9, 2008. Accessed July 23, 2009. Online: http://sitesources.worldbank.org/INTPACIFICISLANDS/Resources/PacificTelcoReport.pdf.

Westermark, George. "Clan Claims: Land, Law and Violence in the Papua New Guinea Eastern Highlands." *Oceania* 67, no. 3 (March 1997) 218–33. Accessed October 17, 2010. Online: http://www.jstor.org/stable/4031558.

White, Ellen G. H. *Counsels to Writers and Editors: A Grouping of Messages of Counsel Addressed to Writers and Editors*. Nashville: Southern Publishing Association, 1946.

Bibliography

Whiteman, Darrell L. "Melanesian Religions: An Overview." In *An Introduction to Melanesian Religions: A Handbook for Church Workers*, edited by Ennio Mantovani, 87–121. Point Series 6. Goroka, PNG: Melanesian Institute, 1984.

WHO. "Maternal Mortality in 2005: Estimates Developed by WHO, UNICEF, UNFPA and the World Bank." Geneva, Switzerland: World Health Organization, 2007. Accessed August 11, 2008. Online: http://www.childinfo.org/files/maternal_mortality_in_2005.pdf.

Williams, William C. "Family Life and Relations." In *Baker Theological Dictionary of the Bible*, edited by Walter A. Elwell, 243–45. Grand Rapids: Baker, 1996.

Young, Robert. *Analytical Concordance to the Bible*. New York: Funk & Wagnalls, 1936.

Zocca, Franco, and Nicholas de Groot. *Young Melanesian Project: Data Analysis*. Point Series 21. Goroka, PNG: Melanesian Institute for Pastoral and Socio-Economic Service, 1997.

Scripture Index

Old Testament

Genesis
1:28	59
2:24	59
14:14	60
39:7–13	59
37–50	63

Leviticus
18, 20	60

Deuteronomy
6:2–7	61, 105
25:5	62

1 Samuel
16–17	63

2 Samuel
	63

2 Samuel
11–12	60

2 Kings
5	63
22	63
23	63

Proverbs
17:6	61

Daniel
	63

Jeremiah
	63

Joel
2:28	62
2:29	62

Malachi
4:5	62
4:6	62

New Testament

Matthew
18:4	64, 105
18:5	64, 105
18:6	64, 105
19:14	64, 105
28	62

Luke
18:16–18	62

John
13:34	62, 105
15:12	62

Romans
5:8	65
8:23	61, 105

Galatians
5:5	105

2 Timothy
3:16	64, 105
3:17	64, 105

Revelation
14:6–12	65
14:8	65
18	68

Name Index

Adler, Alfred, 28
Ahuja, M. L., 41
Anderson, Ray, 105
Andrews, John Nevins, 72
Anivai, Germaine, 9n13
Arnett, Jeffrey J., 26, 30, 103

Bachman, Jerald G., 32
Bartle, Neville, 52, 105
Bartle-Angus, Kathryn, 109
Bell, Goodloe Harper, 73
Bergh, Henry, 75
Berzonsky, Michael D., 31
Brand, Charles F., 108
Brookfield, S. D., 107
Byington, John, 69

Caffarella, Rosemary S., 96–99, 107n9, 119n1
Chowning, Ann, 21, 103
Christ, 50, 61, 62, 64, 65, 66, 92
Clark, Chap, ix, 9, 30, 105

Damaro, Kadasa, 78n16, 87n12, 88, 89, 91
Darius, Matupit, 78n16
Darwin, Charles, 27,
Dean, Kenda Creasy, 30, 105
DeVries, Mark, 106
Dickins, Hugh A., 79, 92
Dickson-Waiko, Anne, 43, 104
Dudley, Roger, 77

Elkind, David, 32n45, 105
Erickson, Matilda, 73
Erikson, Erik, 28, 103

Fenbury, Helen Sheils, 22, 103
Fenner, Harry, 73
Fields, Doug, 106
Fink, L. Dee, 99, 101, 112
Fowler, James W., 104
Freud, Sigmund, 27, 28

Gane, Barry, 77
Gillespie, Bailey, 77
Giris, Jeline, 25, 103
God, ix, 59–67, 70, 71, 75, 86, 87, 91, 97, 105, 124, 125
Goodson, Dale, 50
Gray, Ken, 78, 80
Greenleaf, Floyd, 72n1, 106
Griffen, Vanessa, 104
Groot, Nicholas de, 103

Haeckel, Ernst, 27
Hall, G. Stanley, 26, 27, 30, 31
Hardel, Richard A., 106
Herdt, Gilbert, 20, 103
Hogbin, H. Ian, 21, 25, 103
Holbrook, Robert, 106
Holt, Harriet, 74
Hubbs, Delaura L., 108

Name Index

Jesus, 52, 62, 64–66, 71, 72, 83, 89, 91, 105
Jung, Carl, 28

Kern, Milton E. , 73, 74
Knowles, Malcolm S., 96
Kohlberg, Lawrence, 29, 30, 103
Kwasam, Nathan, 104

Lamarck, Jean, 27
Lansdown, Lewis, 80
Lavaiamat, Daniel, 78n16, 79, 81n24, 83n3
LeFever, Marlene D., 97
Lemke, Mrs., 78
Loughborough, John, 72

Mantovani, Ennio, 49, 105
Matane, Paulias, 20, 41, 103, 104
McCarthy, Bernice, 97
Mead, Margaret, 20, 27, 103
Mueller, Ivo, 18
Mundhenk, Kent, 50

Nietzsche, Friedrich, 27

Pascoe, Marie, 79
Paulsen, Jan, 77
Piaget, Jean, 29, 103

Raethel, Mrs., 78
Rahn, David, 30
Rapaport, Moshe, 104,
Roehlkepartain, Eugene C., 104
Root, Andrew, 105

Rynkiewich, Teresia, 25, 103

Saklo, Aquino, 11n16
Sanders, Arden G., 95
Santrock, John W., 103
Schubert, Branimir, 82, 85
Schwarz, Richard W., 106
Shaw, Daniel, 105
Silva, Kevin, 78, 79, 92
Silva, Thelma, 78n16, 106
Smith, Thomas A., 18
Spaulding, A. W., 74
Spenser, Brenda H., 109
Strommen, Merton P., 106
Sumatau, Tomita, 80

Thornburg, Hershel D., 30
Tindal, Blair, 104
Townsend, Patricia K., 22, 103
Tutty, 79

Vanhoozer, Kelvin J., 105

Wallace Jr., John M., 32
Warren, Luther, 73
Westerhoff III, John H. , 104
White, Ellen G., 66, 72, 107, 124
White, James, 68, 72, 73, 113
Whiteman, Darrell, 105

Yaconelli, Mark, 106
Yani, Ishmael, 15n17

Zocca, Franco, 103

Subject Index

abuse, xii
academic, 40
accident, xii, 48
adolescent, adolescence, 20, 22, 25–32, 44, 51, 83, 103, 104, 122
adoption, xiv, 33, 42, 45–46, 55, 59, 61–62, 70, 112
adult, adulthood, 7, 19, 21–24, 26, 28–31, 33, 46, 64, 78–79, 81, 87, 89, 91, 95–98, 108, 123
Adventist Youth (AY), 76
Adventurers, 81, 113
AIDS, xii, 25, 89, 92, 115
America, 9, 32, 59, 67–68, 71, 74–75, 77, 79–80, 83, 92, 106, 112
aunt, 6–7, 10, 45, 47
Australia, 3, 7, 9, 19, 31, 35–37, 67, 77–79, 83

belief, 30, 45, 49–50, 71, 78, 89, 112
Bible, 3, 14, 52, 59, 60, 62–63, 65–66, 71, 87, 91, 96, 105, 112, 124
billum, 7, 17
bride price, 44
brother, 16, 43, 45, 53, 61–62, 112

challenge, xii-xii, xv, 34, 75, 81, 85–86, 92, 111

child, children, 6–8, 11, 15–26, 28–29, 31, 38, 42–46, 49, 53, 60–62, 64, 66, 69–70, 73, 76, 79, 81, 87–88, 97, 103, 111, 121
childhood, 10, 15, 20–22, 29, 104
Christian, Christianity, 4, 24, 35, 50, 53–55, 61, 67, 75, 88
church, ix, xii-xiv, 5, 25, 44, 51, 54–55, 61–62, 64–92, 95, 97, 99, 106, 108, 112–15, 123
city, xi, xiii, 3–4, 7–10, 35, 41, 54–55, 86–87, 89, 111
clan, xi, 17, 25, 43, 47, 52–53, 60
cognitive development, 29, 32
community xiii, xv, 6, 8, 13, 22, 24–25, 35–36, 42, 44, 46, 51, 61, 66, 71, 74–77, 80, 86–87, 90, 96–97, 104, 112, 115
context, xiii-xiv, 3, 5, 20, 32, 54–55, 68, 71, 95–96, 100–114
course, xiii-xiv, 15, 17, 73, 79, 92, 95–111, 113–15
culture, xii-xiii, 5, 19–20, 24–25, 32, 41, 46–47, 53–54, 59, 64, 67–68, 83, 86–87, 99, 101, 105, 111, 114–15
curriculum, xiii-xiv, 75–76, 92, 101–2, 110–11, 113–14

dance, xi, 5, 21, 23, 42, 54
death, 19–20, 36, 46, 51–53

139

Subject Index

development, xii-xiv, 18-23, 25-32, 36-37, 64, 70, 76, 90, 92, 95-96, 99-100, 102-4, 106, 108, 110-11, 113-14, 121
discipline, 46, 63, 103-4
divorce, xii, 11, 60

ecology, xiii, 34, 54, 100, 111
education, 8, 11-12, 20-21, 24-25, 32, 36-37, 51-52, 66, 70, 74, 76, 79-81, 87-89, 96-99, 104, 108
environment, 19-20, 34, 46, 64, 82, 102, 104, 106, 109-10, 114, 122
eschatology, xiv, 59, 65, 71, 92, 112

family, xi-xii, xiv, 6-18, 24-25, 34, 42-49, 53-55, 59-65, 77, 88, 92, 99, 104-6, 112
father, 6-10, 13-14, 16, 24, 42-43, 51, 53, 60-62, 78
food, 5-10, 12-14, 17-18, 23, 42, 44-45, 49, 54, 70, 88
freedom, 62
Friday Night Fellowship, 80
friend, xi, 16, 18, 38, 40, 45, 48-49, 73, 75, 88, 122
future, 32, 42, 63, 81-85, 89-91, 96-97, 101

gender, 24, 32
General Conference (GC), 69-70, 73-74, 85
goal, xiv, 65, 74, 92, 95, 98, 101-3, 113
governance, xiv, 59, 65, 69, 71, 82-84, 92, 112

highland, xiii, 3-6, 8, 14-15, 18, 41, 54, 80, 111

history, xiv, 17, 59, 62-63, 65, 71-72, 78, 82, 84, 92, 99-100, 102, 106, 110, 112-14, 123

identity, 29-30, 32, 82-83
influence, xii-xiv, 5, 19, 26, 28, 30, 33-35, 38, 48, 54-55, 59, 65, 67-68, 73, 76, 79, 82, 86-87, 89-92, 95, 99-100, 102-4, 110-12, 114, 122
internet, xi-xiv, 35-36, 38-41, 55, 68, 104, 112, 120, 123, 124
island, xiii, 3-5, 7, 11, 13-14, 20, 41, 48, 54, 75, 79, 111, 114

job, 6, 9-11, 26, 39, 48-49
Jones Missionary College, 78
justice, 25, 30, 104

Kambubu, 78, 80
kaukau, 12, 17
King's Heralds, 80
kinship, 45, 48

language, xiii, 3, 5, 14, 20, 22, 41, 47-49, 54, 67, 111
lesson, xiv, 67, 73, 79, 97, 110, 114, 120
life, xii, 5, 7, 9, 13, 16, 19-20, 22, 24-26, 28, 32, 41-42, 45, 48-51, 53-55, 61, 63, 66, 74, 77, 87, 89, 91, 96-97, 100, 112
literature, 42, 67, 76, 99

man, xi, 15, 22, 24, 43, 48, 50, 53, 59, 64, 88, 103, 107
marriage, xii, 25, 42-44, 66, 89, 112
Master Guide, 75-77, 80, 87
media, xii, xiv, 33-37, 54, 68, 70, 85, 88, 91, 99, 104, 112, 122
Medical Cadet Corps (MCC), 75

Subject Index

Melanesia, xiii, 4, 18–20, 22, 25, 42, 50, 52, 96, 99, 103, 111–12, 114–15, 121
men's house, 6, 12–14, 20, 23
menarche, 19, 24, 31
ministry, xiv, 64–65, 69, 74, 92, 96, 106, 112
Missionary Volunteers (MV), 74–75
moral development, 29–30, 32, 104
Morning Watch, 73, 79
mother, xv, 6–10, 12, 15–17, 20, 24, 42–43, 45–46, 53, 60, 78, 89, 112
mumu, 17

New Testament, xiv, 61–62, 64–65, 70, 105, 112

objective, 38, 64, 90, 95, 98–99, 120
Old Testament, xiv, 59, 61, 63–65, 70, 105, 112
organization, 39, 48, 67–69, 73, 76, 81, 96–97

Pacific Adventist University (PAU), 9, 11, 15, 35, 40, 43, 51, 86
Papua New Guinea (PNG), 3, 21–22, 27, 37–41, 49, 80, 90, 104, 115,
parent, xiii, xv, 6, 8, 10–11, 13, 19–20, 23–25, 42–43, 45–46, 49, 61–62, 76, 83, 86–89, 125
pastor, xii–xiii, 55, 78, 95–96, 111, 114
Pathfinder, 68, 74–77, 79–81, 87, 106, 113
payback, 53
physical development, 23
polygamy, 43, 59
president, 69, 76, 85

problem, 13, 25, 29, 32–33, 51–53, 87, 96, 109, 113
psychosocial, xiii, 18–20, 23, 25–26, 29, 99, 102–4, 110–11, 114, 121
publication, 20, 41, 67, 77, 124

relationship, 26, 34, 47, 55, 62, 72, 89–90, 95
religion, 4, 25, 32, 49–52
risk, 46
rites, 20–21, 24, 31, 51, 111
root, xiv, 26–27, 48, 65, 83, 112

Sabbath, xiv, xv, 16, 67, 70, 73, 75, 78–80, 84, 87–88, 113
sanguma, 53, 54
Seventh-day Adventist (SDA), xiv, 5, 54–55, 65, 67–72, 74, 77–78, 80–83, 87, 89, 92, 99, 100, 106–7, 112–14
sex, xii, 20–21, 28, 32, 60, 89, 105
sister, 16–17, 43, 45, 62, 112
social, 19–21, 23, 25, 27–30, 32, 40, 43, 48, 50, 82, 85, 87, 97, 104, 122
society, xii-xiv, 3, 9, 19, 22–27, 30–32, 60, 62, 68, 73–74, 81–82, 88–89, 91, 95–96, 99–100, 103, 111–12
Sonoma, 80
sorcery, 7, 50, 52–55, 88
spiritual, spirituality, 19, 49–50, 52, 63, 73, 81, 88, 91, 102–4, 110, 114, 121
spirit, 49–53, 61–62, 87
STORMCo, 76
student, xiv, 9, 11, 15, 33, 40, 43–44, 46–48, 50–52, 75, 80–81, 86, 95–103, 105–10, 113–14, 120–25
suicide, xii, 32, 88–89, 115

141

Subject Index

theology, xiii-xiv, 50, 54–55, 59, 71, 92, 102, 105, 110, 112, 114, 124
tribe, 25, 50, 60–61
Valuegenesis, 77
village, xiii, 3, 5–7, 9–10, 13–15, 17, 20, 23, 26, 36, 38–39, 42–43, 46–48, 53–55, 79, 87, 89, 111, 113

wantok, xiv, 40, 47–49, 55, 104, 112
Western, xii-xiv, 8–9, 15, 18–20, 25–26, 35, 48, 52–54, 67, 84
woman, 6, 12, 19, 22–23, 25–26, 43–44, 53, 59–60, 75, 82–83, 85, 89, 91

women's house, 6
worldview, xiii, 3, 5, 18, 50–52, 54, 55, 85, 98, 111

youth, xii, xiii, xiv, 22, 25, 30, 32–33, 35, 42, 54–55, 62–65, 68, 70, 72–92, 96, 98–106, 109, 110–15, 122–25
youth ministry, xiii, xiv, 34, 54–55, 59–60, 62, 64–66, 68–69, 71–72, 78, 80, 91–92, 95–96, 98–102, 105–6, 108–14, 123–25
youth worker, xiii, 89, 111, 114, 123